45 Tang Time – Tang and Yuan Dynasty, China
46 The Final Firecracker – The Mongol Invasions
47 Underwear, Wind, and Water – Medieval Science
48 Pick-and-Mix – Southeast Asia from 500 to 1300 A.D.
50 Pyramid Crazy – The Mayas

CHAPTER FOUR
GETTING TO KNOW YOU

52 World Map and Introduction
54 Timeline: 1300–1650
56 Come to Think of It – A Wave of Invention
58 Fleas and Florins – The Rebirth of Europe
60 Hello Sailor – The Age of Exploration
61 Poles and Parties – European Nation-States
62 Joggers and Scrubbers – Aztecs and Incas
64 Mongol, Ming, and Manchu – China from 1368–1644 A.D.
65 "Cannon" Law – Korea and Thailand
66 Founding and Sikhing – Mogul India
67 Mighty Muslims – The Rise of the Ottoman and Safanid Empires
68 Market Forces – African Kingdoms: Mali, Songhai, Ndongo, and Zimbabwe

CHAPTER FIVE
THE SHAPE OF THINGS TO COME

70 World Map and Introduction
72 Timeline: 1650–1800
74 Buzzing – Native Americans and the Colonies
76 Traders and Floggers – Africa in the 18th century: the Ashanti, the Arabs, and Slavery
78 Rolling Around – The Decline of the Safanid and Mogul Empires, the Rise of the Marathas
80 Eastern Promise – Qing China, Australia
82 Sparks – 17th- and 18th-century Europe
84 Rights, Wrongs, and Revolutions – The American and French Revolutions
86 Steaming Through the Daffodils – The Agricultural and early Industrial Revolutions

CHAPTER SIX
STEAMING ON

88 World Map and Introduction
90 Timeline: 1800–1914
92 Brainy's New Buddy – Industrial Revolution
94 Napoléon and Co. – 19th-century Europe and the birth of Italy and Germany
96 Carving the Turkey – The Decline of the Ottoman Empire
98 North and South – The Civil War, the Revolutions in South America and Mexico
100 Greedy Feeders – The Scramble for Africa
102 Joining the Barbarians – Qing China in decline, the Rise of Japan
104 Happy Campers – The end of the 19th century: the buildup to World War I, Arts and Crafts

CHAPTER SEVEN
HOPES AND FEARS

106 World Map and Introduction
108 Timeline: 20th Century
110 Wartime – World War I
111 Jazz Time – The 1920s
112 Red Lights – The Russian and Chinese Revolutions
114 Flash... – The Rise of Fascism
115 ...and Grab – World War II
116 Democrats and Commies – The Cold War
118 Competition Time – The Global Market
120 Jeans and Greens – People in the 20th century, Looking after our planet
122 Tiger Time – The Eastern Tigers, The World in the 1990s

EPILOGUE

124 Still Smiling What next for the super-brainy people?
126 Index

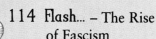

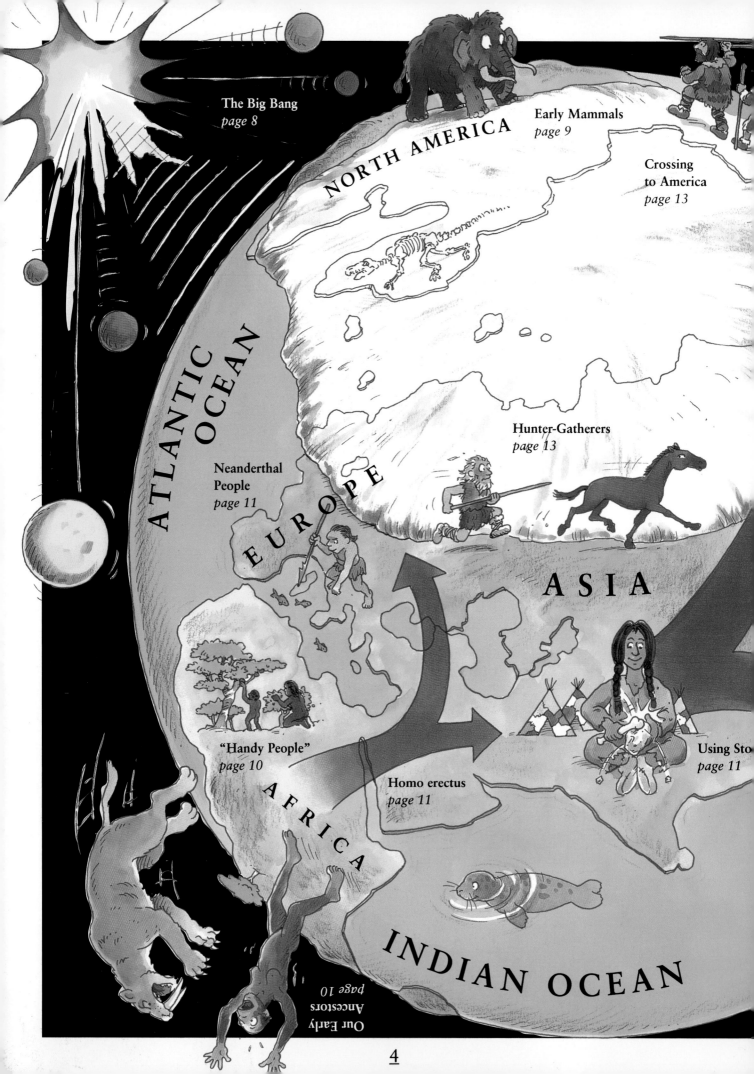

The Big Bang
page 8

Early Mammals
page 9

Crossing
to America
page 13

NORTH AMERICA

ATLANTIC OCEAN

Neanderthal
People
page 11

Hunter-Gatherers
page 13

EUROPE

ASIA

"Handy People"
page 10

Homo erectus
page 11

Using Sto
page 11

AFRICA

Our Early
Ancestors
page 10

INDIAN OCEAN

4

AND THEN...

A HISTORY OF THE WORLD

Written by Stewart Ross
Illustrated by John Lobban, Alison Atkins, and Mark Peppé

COPPER BEECH BOOKS
BROOKFIELD, CONNECTICUT

AND THEN...

is the first really clever history of the world. Everything that ever happened – all the important parts, anyway – is presented in bite-sized chunks to suit all tastes.

The chapters are divided into spreads, each of which focuses on a particular region or topic. They are also introduced by a world map, which helps you to find what you're looking for, and a time line, to show what was happening at the same time in different parts of the world.

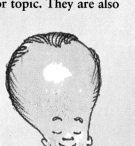

© Aladdin Books Ltd 1996
© Text: Stewart Ross/Aladdin Books Ltd 1996

Designed and produced by
Aladdin Books Ltd
28 Percy Street
London W1P 0LD

First published in the United States in 1996 by
Copper Beech Books,
an imprint of The Millbrook Press
2 Old New Milford Road
Brookfield, Connecticut 06804

Editor Jim Pipe
Designed by David West Children's Books
Designer Simon Morse
Illustrators John Lobban, Alison Atkins, Mark Peppé

Printed in Belgium

This book is dedicated to John Lobban and Rosie Morse

Library of Congress
Cataloging-in-Publication Data

Ross, Stewart.
    And then— : a history of the world in 119½ pages / by Stewart
    Ross : illustrated by John Lobban, Alison Atkins, and Mark Peppé.
        p. cm.
    Includes index.
    Summary: A history of the world, with sections on famous people, important inventions, bizarre facts, and comparisons among different cultures.
    ISBN 0-7613-0531-9 (lib. bdg.). — ISBN 0-7613-0508-4 (pbk.)
    1. World history—Juvenile literature. [1. World history.]
I. Lobban, John, ill. II. Title.
D20.R84 1996
909—dc20   96-2330
                                             CIP AC

CONTENTS

CHAPTER ONE
BANGS, BRAINS, AND BREADMAKERS

4 World Map and Introduction
6 Timeline: 20,000 mya to 5000 B.C.
8 The Big Bang – Early Life and Dinosaurs
10 Pluckers and Pokers – The First People
12 March of the Bigheads – Hunter-Gatherers
14 Settling Down – The Spread of Farming

CHAPTER TWO
FROM DIGGERS TO DOERS

16 World Map and Introduction
18 Timeline: 5000 B.C.–500 A.D.
20 Waterworks – The First Civilizations
21 Land of the Hippo-Croc – Ancient Egypt
22 Making China – Ancient China
23 Caste Masters
      Ancient India
24 Bashers and Knockers
      Africa up to 500 A.D.
25 Doing it Their Way
      The Early Americans
26 Marooned – Japan and the Pacific Islands
27 Party Time – The First Inventions
28 War, Gore, and Armies – Mycenae and Crete
29 Left Out in the Cold – The Celts
30 League Leaders – Ancient Greece and Persia
31 The Doers – Ancient Rome
32 Zap-gods and Holy Men – Early Religion

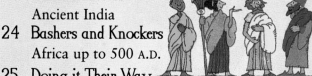

CHAPTER THREE
HALFTIME

34 World Map and Introduction
36 Timeline: 500–1300 A.D.
38 The Great Pushover – The Fall of Rome
40 Camels and Caliphs – The Conquering Arabs
42 Culture Cake – Emerging African Kingdoms
43 Rome Again – The Byzantine Empire
44 Belly Buttons and Salesmen – Gupta India

1 AND THEN...

BANGS, BRAINS, AND BREADMAKERS

We haven't been around long. Not in galactic terms, anyway...
Imagine a large, very slow clock. On this clock 1½
normal years is about one second. So a person lives about
45–50 seconds and a century is a minute. According to
the clock, Christopher Columbus crossed the Atlantic Ocean five
minutes ago. It is only 15 minutes since Julius Caesar was
alive and the first civilization began 45 minutes before that.
On the same time scale, there have been
human-like creatures for about three
weeks. Our remotest ancestors
appeared some seven months
ago. The world is just under a
century old.

In other words, civilized
humans have been around for only the
last hour of a 100-year story.

This chapter deals with the previous 99 years, 364
days, and 11 hours. It covers all the really important parts of the Earth's
history, from creation to civilization. In order to get to modern humans we
have to survive the Big Bang... wade through primeval slime... avoid
being trampled on by dinosaurs... and make sure not to
take the wrong path down one of evolution's millions
of dead ends. So get ready for the longest, most
fantastic journey of all time – through all time!

**Paddling to
Australia**
page 13

The First Farmers
pages 14–15

20,000 MYA TO 5000 B.C.

PREHISTORY

40,000   20,000

mya = million years ago   ya = years ago

20,000 mya
The Big Bang

4,600 mya
Earth formed

3,500 mya
Life appears on Earth.

PALEOZOIC ERA
570–245 mya

Cambrian Period
570–510 mya –
Trilobites and jawless fish evolve, all animals still live in the sea.

Ordovician Period
510–435 mya – *First animals with backbones (fish) appear.*

Silurian Period
435–410 mya – *Fish develop jaws, plants appear on land.*

Devonian Period
410–360 mya – *"Age of Fishes." Sharks, insects, and amphibians appear.*

Carboniferous Period
360–290 mya – *First reptiles, swampy forests grow, giant insects.*

Permian Period 290–245 mya – *Seed plants.*

MESOZOIC ERA
245–65 mya

Triassic Period
245–208 mya – *First turtles, crocodiles, dinosaurs, sea/flying reptiles, and mammals.*

Jurassic Period 208–144 mya – *First birds, dinosaurs at their biggest size.*

Cretaceous Period
144–65 mya – *Horned and armored dinosaurs, flowering plants.*

CENOZOIC ERA
65 mya–present

First primates *(animals with grasping hands)* **32 mya**

Proconsuls 25 mya *human ancestors (left)*

Australopithecus 5–1.5 mya
Early humans used sticks and stones found lying around as tools, walked upright, mainly vegetarian.

Homo habilis 2–0.5 mya
First early humans to make stone tools.

Homo erectus
1.5–0.5 mya – *First humans to move out of Africa and with larger brain. Learns to make fire, hunt large animals, talks?, make shelters and chopping tools.*

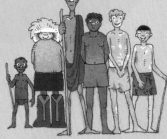

Homo sapiens 500,000 ya to present – *biggest brain yet, first clothes, burial sites, etc.*

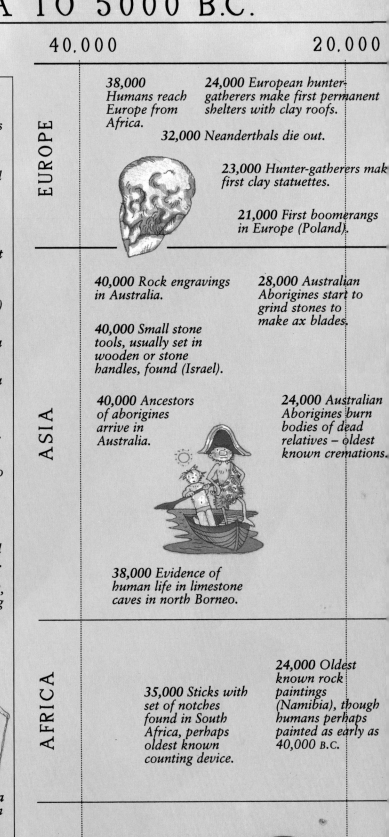

EUROPE

38,000 Humans reach Europe from Africa.

24,000 European hunter-gatherers make first permanent shelters with clay roofs.

32,000 Neanderthals die out.

23,000 Hunter-gatherers mak first clay statuettes.

21,000 First boomerangs in Europe (Poland).

ASIA

40,000 Rock engravings in Australia.

40,000 Small stone tools, usually set in wooden or stone handles, found (Israel).

40,000 Ancestors of aborigines arrive in Australia.

38,000 Evidence of human life in limestone caves in north Borneo.

28,000 Australian Aborigines start to grind stones to make ax blades.

24,000 Australian Aborigines burn bodies of dead relatives – oldest known cremations.

AFRICA

35,000 Sticks with set of notches found in South Africa, perhaps oldest known counting device.

24,000 Oldest known rock paintings (Namibia), though humans perhaps painted as early as 40,000 B.C.

AMERICA

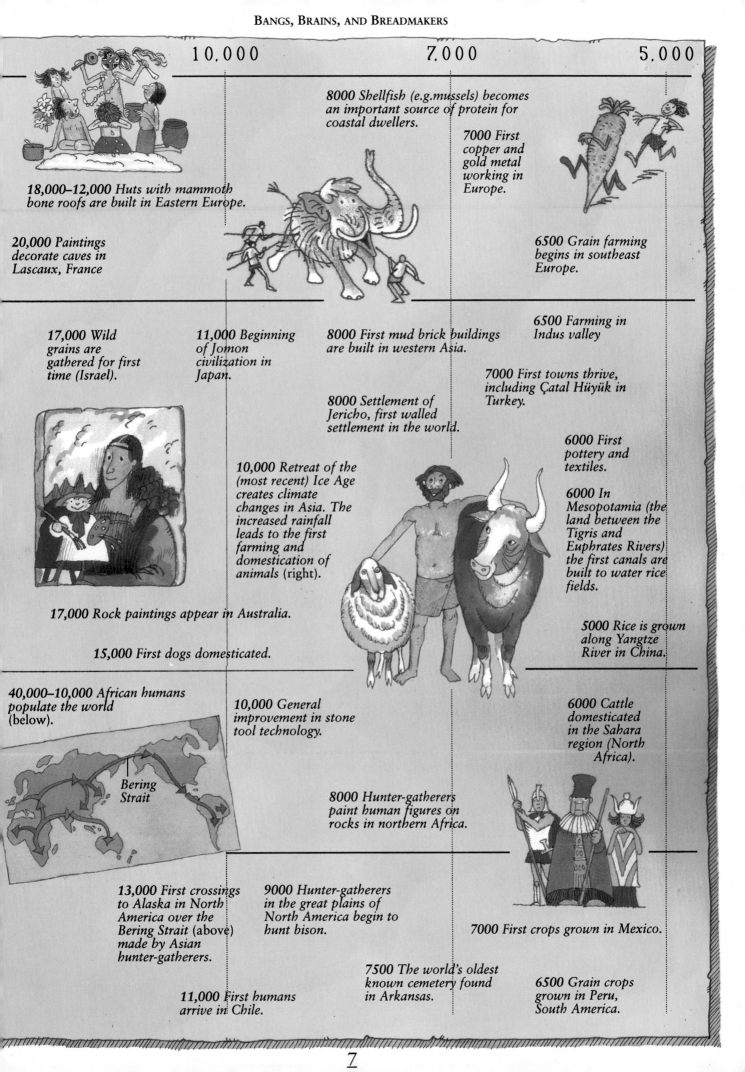

10.000   7.000   5.000

8000 Shellfish (e.g.mussels) becomes an important source of protein for coastal dwellers.

7000 First copper and gold metal working in Europe.

18,000–12,000 Huts with mammoth bone roofs are built in Eastern Europe.

20,000 Paintings decorate caves in Lascaux, France

6500 Grain farming begins in southeast Europe.

17,000 Wild grains are gathered for first time (Israel).

11,000 Beginning of Jomon civilization in Japan.

8000 First mud brick buildings are built in western Asia.

6500 Farming in Indus valley

7000 First towns thrive, including Çatal Hüyük in Turkey.

8000 Settlement of Jericho, first walled settlement in the world.

6000 First pottery and textiles.

10,000 Retreat of the (most recent) Ice Age creates climate changes in Asia. The increased rainfall leads to the first farming and domestication of animals (right).

6000 In Mesopotamia (the land between the Tigris and Euphrates Rivers) the first canals are built to water rice fields.

17,000 Rock paintings appear in Australia.

5000 Rice is grown along Yangtze River in China.

15,000 First dogs domesticated.

40,000–10,000 African humans populate the world (below).

10,000 General improvement in stone tool technology.

6000 Cattle domesticated in the Sahara region (North Africa).

Bering Strait

8000 Hunter-gatherers paint human figures on rocks in northern Africa.

13,000 First crossings to Alaska in North America over the Bering Strait (above) made by Asian hunter-gatherers.

9000 Hunter-gatherers in the great plains of North America begin to hunt bison.

7000 First crops grown in Mexico.

7500 The world's oldest known cemetery found in Arkansas.

6500 Grain crops grown in Peru, South America.

11,000 First humans arrive in Chile.

THE BIG BANG

Sun

Earth

This was the Big Bang. According to the Expanding Universe theory, the pieces are still zooming around.

In a matter of seconds, apparently, countless "toffee particles" cooled and stuck together in lumps. These lumps became the stars and planets. About 4,600 mya, near an ordinary star known as the "Sun," an unusual planet turned up. We call it "Earth."

Hot gas ball   Boring golf ball

For some 1,000 million years the Earth was bleak and boring, like the moon today except much hotter. Then something remarkable – possibly unique – happened. Life appeared (about 3,500 mya). Nobody knows what sparked it off – possibly a lucky mix of chemicals in a sunny rock pool.

There are all sorts of explanations for the origins of life, the universe, and everything. Some are mythical, some religious, some scientific. Since no one was around at the time, we'll never know for sure what really happened.

Some scientists now believe that at first there was a lump of hot, dense "something" – like a glowing slab of super-galactic "toffee." About 20,000 million years ago (mya), this "toffee" exploded into zillions of pieces that zoomed out into nothingness.

The creatures were not much to look at, just bugs and algae. But they were alive. From them developed all the amazing animals that make our world so special. As you can imagine, it took quite an effort to get from pond slime to pop singers. It took evolution 3,250 million years just to come up with backbones.

8

The first steps were the hardest. By 570 mya, a range of complex creatures and plants had emerged.

This proved to be a false start, for an Ice Age wiped a lot of them out (*above*).

In about 245 mya, evolution was trying again. This time it got as far as small mammals, birds, and – most famous of all – dinosaurs.

Looking Earthy
220 mya

From Gas to Garden!
Over millions of years the Earth turned from a ball of gas into a living planet.

Almost there
66 mya

During the age of reptiles, officially called the Mesozoic or Middle Era, the Earth's single landmass started to break up into separate continents (*above*). These then floated around like pieces of ice on a pond until they ended up in roughly the same location as today.

Happily – or sadly if you were a dinosaur – the reptile age was a second false start.

Something happened to alter the Earth's climate and the giant lizards died out. Evolution took a deep breath and made a third attempt in the Cenozoic or recent era (65 mya to present).

It was mammals' turn to dominate. They came in all shapes and sizes, from mice to mammoths. The primates (animals that can grasp with their hands) came about 32 mya, followed 7 million years later by small monkey-like creatures known as Proconsuls (*left*).

Like it or not, these Proconsuls were our distant relatives.

Lizard Lords
Dinosaurs ruled the world for over 150 million years!

Bombed Out
What happened to the dinosaurs? They may have died out when a giant meteor crashed into the Earth. This had roughly the same impact as a nuclear war.

Vast dust clouds rose into the air, blocking out the sun and dramatically altering the climate. This was more than the dim-witted dinosaurs could cope with and they faded away. Another recent theory is that they died of cancer (below)!

PLUCKERS AND POKERS

About 4½ mya creatures that looked a lot like us began to emerge. These were the hominids. They walked around on two legs, leaving their nimble hands free for carrying, fighting, or simply scratching themselves.

Hominids had big, meat-chewing jaws and sharp eyesight. Their most unusual feature was a large brain – about the same size as the engine of a powerful motorcycle.

By piecing together hominid remains, experts have concluded that they came in various shapes and sizes.

The two we know best are the unpronounceable "Australopithecine" and the "Homo," which means simply "human." The long-winded Australopithecines died out. But – fortunately for us – the Homo did not!

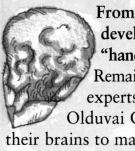

From the ordinary Homo developed Homo habilis, or "handy person" (2–1½ mya). Remains of these first manual experts, found in the East African Olduvai Gorge, tell us that they used their brains to make shelters and tools (*left*).

The idea of a shelter was no big deal – even birds had nests – but tools were something different. The first tools were just shaped lumps of stone used for bashing and scraping – not brilliant, but an important first step on the 2½-million-year-road to the can-opener.

The next important move was out of Africa. The creature that made it was Homo erectus, meaning an upright type of Homo. Erectus had a large forehead, like Frankenstein's monster (*page 93*), and a brain the size of a small car engine (1000 cc).

NAME DROPPING
The most complete Australopithecine skeleton (about 40 percent of it) was found in East Africa. It was about 3 million years old.
The excavators considered the name "Australopithecine" a bit awkward, so they called her Lucy. Why? Because at the time they were listening to the Beatles' song Lucy in the Sky With Diamonds!

They're Off!
The small-car-brained Erectuses leave Africa to populate the world.

Tooltastic
*Homo erectus
specialized in wooden
and bone spears and bowls.*

Homo erectus flourished in Africa, Asia, and Europe about 1¹/₂-¹/₂ mya. It's not easy to tell from pieces of old bone and stone what it got up to, but it seems to have been much more human than its ancestors. It made larger and better tools, lived in large family units in what we call "home bases" (sometimes actual buildings), and joined with others for big game hunting. It used fire and may even have dabbled in art.

FIRE POWER
Homo erectus wasn't bright enough to make fire, but it learned how to use it once it was going. This was perhaps the species' most important discovery.

Firelight enabled the Erectus family to take up residence in the local cave. Flames provided central heating, scared away wild beasts, and cooked their food. This allowed them to eat tough meat and bitter plants.

Evidence from the Transvaal (South Africa) and China suggests that the Erectuses were using fire-power about ¹/₂ mya.

*Homo sapiens
neanderthalensis*

Homo sapiens sapiens

Homo sapiens (almost us!) appeared some 500,000 years ago. The new species was not very different from Homo erectus, just brighter. For 400,000 years it continued to develop along the same lines as its ancestors.

Toward the end of this period the species evolved into Homo sapiens neanderthalensis (or Neanderthals) and Homo sapiens sapiens, or modern humans. In time the strongly-built, mammoth-hunting Neanderthals died out, leaving only Homo sapiens sapiens.

At last, we had arrived!

THE MARCH OF THE BIGHEADS

Homo sapiens means "brainy person," so Homo sapiens sapiens means "brainy brainy person" or "super-brainy person." Since we gave ourselves this show-off name, a better translation might be "big-headed-person."

No one is quite sure how, why, or where Homo sapiens got the extra bit of sapiens that turned them into modern humans.

It all happened very slowly, of course. Some scientists think we first turned up in Africa, then wandered off into Europe and Asia, evolving different shapes and colors as we went. All the major racial groups had appeared by about 10,000 B.C. (*left*). Others say we evolved separately in three continents, so looked slightly different from the start. Wherever we came from, by about 40,000 B.C. we were going strong.

MEANWHILE...

Evolution is a maze with many more dead ends than ways through. One such dead end was Homo sapiens neanderthalensis, or the Neanderthals. These beefy and possibly hairy people lived in Europe and Asia about 120,000–35,000 years ago, during the last Ice Age.

They buried their dead, ate their enemies' brains, and may have learned to talk. But while Homo sapiens sapiens was spreading out over the planet, their Neanderthal cousins fizzled out. Maybe they had not eaten enough brains!

Pigs grunt, birds sing, whales wo-o-o-o-w, but only humans have words. It is possible that language made modern humans – for example, by learning to talk old Homo sapiens put themselves into the evolutionary fast lane. It's good to talk!

As there are 30 groups of languages, language may have started in several places at about the same time (no one knows when). Once in use, language allowed knowledge and ideas to be passed down through generations.

Boaring! Back to gathering nuts and berries again.

Huh! Humans are all brains and no brawn

March of the Bigheads 40,000– 10,000

Language led to ideas. In our spare time, we wondered about who we were and what we were doing. Out of such idle thought grew art, mathematics, science, politics, and religion.

Humans were painting on cave walls in Africa over 25,000 years ago. Ten thousand years later their French relatives armed themselves with lamps of burning animal fat and began decorating the caves in their area (*above*). No one knows why they suddenly stopped. A prehistoric power outage?

Humans probably first buried dead bodies to get rid of the smell. By 15,000 B.C. they were leaving useful things like cups in the grave (*right*). This wasn't forgetfulness, but kindness: The body might need a drink when it came alive again.

Why were other bodies buried with their legs tucked under them? Whatever the answer, we were now considering life after death. In other words, we were religious.

The chattering species was a hunter-gatherer. To survive it needed animals to kill and fruits and nuts to collect. The search for these things took it all over the world.

BOILED GRANDMA
Early peoples did not always bury their dead. The Massagetae, for example, killed their elderly folk, boiled them, and ate them. Most of them, anyway.

Travel was easier because the polar ice caps had grown during the last Ice Age (about 110,000 –10,000 B.C.), leaving the oceans about 300 ft lower than today. The inhabitants of Asia could cross to America without getting their feet wet and paddle to Australia across 60 miles of shallow water.

Boats were just one of the inventions Homo sapiens sapiens dreamed up (page 27). They also produced clothes, harpoons, needles, counting sticks, the bow and arrow, and the first human-made material, a mix of bone and clay for pots.

Finally, as the Ice Age melted away and the well-watered Earth sprouted all kinds of delicious plants, we made the biggest discovery of all. Dig up the earth a bit in the fall, throw in a handful of seeds, keep away the weeds and the birds and – hey presto! – next year's food grows up out of the ground as if by magic.

Humans had learned to farm (9000 B.C.).

SETTLING DOWN

Nowadays, we are used to changes happening very quickly all over the world at the same time. In the past it was not like this.

It took thousands of years for farming to catch on, and in some parts of the world hunter-gatherers survived into modern times.

There are two sides to farming: growing crops and tending animals. Between about 15,000 B.C. and 3000 B.C., millions of people, especially in the Near and Far East, mastered both.

It all began with dogs.
Roughly 17,000 years ago, dogs – or dog-like wolves – realized it was much more pleasant to work with humans than against them. Humans agreed, and the partnership has been going strong ever since.

Sumerian (page 20) sheep joined in about 9000 B.C. Goats, cows, and other beasts trooped into the farmyard over the next thousand years.

Humans were now King of the Species.
To prove it, they employed other animals as servants. Camels, asses, donkeys, oxen, llamas, and finally horses became their beasts of burden.

ANIMAL TRACTORS
The first plow was just a stick or antler used to loosen the soil before planting. Two-person plows appeared in about 7000 B.C. The puller heaved it along on a rope while a lazy friend leaned on it to make sure it cut into the soil (main picture).

This went on for thousands of years until the exhausted puller finally gave up and handed over the rope to an ox. Animal plowing, found in the Middle East by about 3000 B.C., improved the crop yield – and farmers' tempers.

LOAD

CART

AXLE

WHEEL

NEW YOKE, NEW YORK
For thousands of years the cart was the best way to move heavy goods on land.

Wheels were first used in Sumeria. They were brilliant for making round pots and for ox carts (which appeared in about 6000 B.C.), but they took a while to catch on: The Chinese hoofed it for another 4,000 years.

The land bridge between Asia and America had now submerged, so Americans stayed wheel-free for another 3,500 years.

Like other animals, humans were always on the lookout for a free meal.

In about 9000 B.C., some non-hunting types started harvesting wild crops.

The Asians discovered cultivation 3,000 years later, harvesting the rice they had planted and tended.

IS AY UP

YOKE

OX

Agriculture changed humans more than any other discovery.

Before it we were pig-sticking, berry-picking wanderers, jacks-of-all-trades – not so different from other animals.

Afterward we were house-dwelling, law-making specialists, living as no other creatures had lived before.

Agriculture developed in a fertile boomerang between the Tigris and Euphrates Rivers.

Tigris River

Euphrates River

MEANWHILE...
While Asians and Europeans galloped around on horseback and had their loads pulled by horse and cart, Americans had to make do with lazy llamas.

Horses and camels had crossed to America during the Ice Ages. But instead of learning to ride the creatures, as others did in the rest of the world, Americans continued to eat them!

Not that the Europeans were terribly conservation-minded. At about the same time as Americans carved up their last horse (5000 B.C.), the Europeans dived into a final helping of mammoth stew.

Agriculture produced plenty of food.
As more mouths could be fed, the population rose. Not everyone was required to work in the fields, so potters and carpenters set up workshops. Single farmsteads grew to hamlets. Mud-brick villages and even larger settlements appeared.

The pompous bosses of community life muscled in – soldiers, governors, and priests (*above*). Humans had been struggling to get their act together for 5 million years. By about 5000 B.C., with the help of seeds and a few sheep, they had become *almost* civilized.

2 AND THEN...

FROM DIGGERS TO DOERS

Civilization did not begin on a tropical island, where the living was easy. It began on the banks of five great rivers – the Tigris, Euphrates, Nile, Indus, and Yellow. Between swirling waters and barren uplands, the going was tough – and the tough got going. They learned to work together or die. Many followed the idea of you-scratch-my-field-and-I'll-scratch-yours.

Greek Gods
page 33

The Celts
page 29

Early Inventions
page 27

Ancient Rome
page 31

ATLANTIC OCEAN

EUROPE

A

Ancient Greece
page 30

AFRICA

Ancient Egypt
page 21

Early African Civilizations
page 24

The First Armies
page 28

Ancient Sumeria
page 20

The number of super-brainy people rose from (roughly) 90 million in early Egyptian times (about 4000 B.C.) to 130 million at the time of Julius Caesar (100–44 B.C.). More brains meant more ideas and discoveries, especially in the cities. Trade brought wealth, leisure, jealousy, and war. Because they were pushed around by priests, kings and councils, fewer people could do their own thing. The civilization craze did not catch on everywhere. Beyond the farmlands, away from the stone-bronze-iron triple jump, hunter-gatherers went on trapping and plucking just as they had done for the previous 10,000 years. Sadly, where farmers and wandering hunter-gatherers met, the wanderers fared much worse.

The First Americans
page 25

Early Civilization in the Pacific
page 26

Buddhism
page 23

Ancient China
page 22

Ancient India
page 23

Confucius
page 32

Confucius says... Read on!

5000 B.C. to 500 A.D.

5000	3000	1000	800	600

ASIA

4000 Bronze is first cast in Near East.

3500 Invention of wheel in Sumeria.

3500 Foundation of city of Ur in Sumeria.

3500 First use of animals to pull plows.

3100 Pictographic writing invented in Sumeria.

2750 Growth of civilizations in Indus Valley, Pakistan.

2334–2279 King Sargon of Akkad founds first empire in world history.

2700 Gilgamesh rules at Uruk in Sumer.

2200 Jomon civilization reaches its peak in Japan.

1790–1750 King Hammurabi creates Babylonian Empire.

1600 Shang Bronze Age in China.

1000 King David unites Israel and Judea.

1200 Beginning of Jewish religion.

1450 Indian Vedas composed.

650 First coins (left) in Lydia (Asia Minor).

650 Early iron working in China.

721–627 Assyria's Empire at its greatest.

EUROPE

4000 Farming reaches Britain from Europe.

3500–2000 Construction of huge stone tombs and circles in France, Spain, and Britain.

3000 First bronze in Crete.

3000 Spread of copperworking.

1600–1100 Mycenean civilization in Greece.

2000–1450 Minoan civilization in Crete (right).

1100 Phoenicians develop alphabet.

1100–700 Spread of Phoenicians around Mediterranean.

776 First Olympic Games held in Greece.

753 Traditional date for founding of Rome.

AFRICA

4500 Pottery made in Nubia (North Africa).

4000 Farming peoples in Sahara domesticate animals.

3500 Sail invented in Egypt.

2600 Cheops builds great pyramid at Giza, Egypt.

2500 Building of Sphinx at Giza, Egypt.

3100 King Menes unites upper and lower Egypt.

1000–300 Kingdom of Kushites flourishes.

900 Noks in Nigeria work with terracotta (left).

814 Traditional date for founding of Carthage founded by Phoenicians.

671 Egypt overrun by Assyrians.

AMERICA

5000 Maize first cultivated in Mexico.

3500 Cotton used as crop in Peru.

3500 Llama first used as pack animal in Peru.

3000 First pottery in Americas.

2000 First metalworking in Peru.

2000 Inuits settle the Arctic.

1200 Rise of Chavins on Peruvian coast.

900–300 Chavín civilization at Chavín de Huantar in Peru (below).

1150 Beginning of Olmecs in Mexico.

400   **0**   **400**   **600**

550 Cyrus the Great founds Persian Empire.

500 Caste system set up in India.

563–486 Life of Siddhartha Gautama, the Buddha.

479 Death of Confucius (right).

550 Zoroastrianism becomes official religion of Persia.

334–326 Greek Alexander the Great (right) conquers Egypt, Persia, and reaches India.

322 Chandaragupta sets up Mauryan Empire.

221 Qin Shi Huangdi of Qin Dynasty unites China.

262 Asoka, Mauryan Emperor, converts to Buddhism.

202 B.C.–**220** A.D. Han Dynasty rules in China.

214 Qin complete Great Wall of China.

105 First use of paper in China.

150 Buddhism reaches China.

200 Indian epic poems – Mahabharata and Ramayana – written.

270 Magnetic compass in use in China.

224–651 Sassanid Dynasty rules in Persia (right).

300 Stirrup invented in Asia.

320 Chandara Gupta founds Gupta Empire in North India.

520 Decimal system invented in India.

589–617 Sui Dynasty rules in China.

467 End of Gupta Empire.

479–338 Period of classical Greek culture – poetry, drama, sculpture, history, medicine, philosophy, and architecture.

510 Foundation of Roman Republic.

508 Democracy established in Athens.

431–404 Peloponnesian War between Athens and Sparta.

490–479 Persian invasion of Greece defeated at battles of Marathon, Salamis, and Plataea.

338 Macedon controls Greece.

290 Rome completes conquest of Italy.

146 Greece under Roman control.

47–45 B.C. Civil war in Rome, Julius Caesar becomes sole leader.

30 A.D. Jesus of Nazareth crucified in Jerusalem.

27 B.C. Augustus becomes first Roman Emperor.

117 Roman Empire at its greatest extent.

410 Visigoths invade Italy and sack Rome.

313 Christianity first tolerated in Roman Empire.

330 Capital of Roman Empire moves to Constantinople.

---

500 Iron-making techniques spread to sub-saharan Africa.

500–200 Noks begin to use iron.

264–146 Rome defeats Carthage, winning Spain and North Africa.

325 Aksumites destroy Kushite kingdom of Meroe (left).

100 Rise of Aksumite Kingdom of Ethiopia.

30 B.C. Death of Cleopatra, Egypt becomes a Roman province.

---

500 First hieroglyphic writing in Mexico.

300 Rise of Maya civilization.

100 A.D. Mogollon culture flourishes (right).

300 B.C.–**700** A.D. Hopewell people in North America.

300 Start of Teotihuacán civilization in Mexico.

500 Adena civilization at its height in North America.

100 B.C. Hohokam culture begins in North America.

WATERWORKS

Civilization begins

– more or less – when many people settle in one place and learn to get along.

The first town was Çatal Hüyük (Turkey), a honeycomb of mud houses without streets built in 7000 B.C. The front doors were in the roof and dead relatives were shoved under the floor. After 2,000 years, the Çatalhüyükians moved out, perhaps due to the smell!

The Sumerians, furry-skirted farmers

living between the Tigris and Euphrates Rivers, started the first civilization (5000 B.C.). Like other early people, they were obsessed with channeling water into their fields of wheat, barley, and millet. Their civilization was one giant waterworks, with the king as waterworks manager.

The Sumerians built fine cities, such as Ur and Uruk,

which were bigger and less smelly (and easier to say) than Çatal Hüyük.

They also invented things, such as glass, wheels (including the potter's wheel), alcohol, math, writing, and an inaccurate calendar.

The Ziggurat of Ur
The Sumerians' most famous temple looked like a huge pile of bricks.

Then came the Babylonians.

Hammurabi, the mightiest Babylonian king (1790–1750 B.C.), ruled Mesopotamia and wrote the world's first code of laws on stone pillars and clay tablets. The laws were fair but tough (i.e. if you break my leg, I'll break yours).

WHAT-A-MESH
The first recorded name is Gilgamesh, the Sumerian Lord of Uruk. In a gloomy epic, written about 2000 B.C., he struggles against the gods – and loses. In the process the whole world is flooded (the ultimate Sumerian nightmare).

Other Babylonian brain **waves included sewage pipes** (more waterworks) and dividing a circle into 360 degrees and an hour into 60 minutes. But Babylonian laws, pipes, and math could not stop conquest by iron-wielding Hittites in the second millenium B.C. (one millenium=one thousand years).

THE LAND OF THE HIPPO-CROC

About 5,000 years ago, hippos wandered around the Sahara, which was then a grassy place where herds of cattle munched happily beside flowing rivers. But the desert moved in and soon there was only sand and dry bones.

Only the Nile didn't dry up, and beside it the Egyptian civilization appeared. Egypt got its act together a little later than Sumeria. Like the Sumerians, the Egyptians dug to live: agriculture = waterworks = civilization. The first picture of Menes, Egypt's earliest king (3100 B.C.), shows him digging a ditch (*top*).

Mummy's Boys
Dead pharaohs were bandaged up and stuffed into big coffins (called sarcophagi).

MEANWHILE...
Roughly when the Egyptians were drawing doll-like figures (hieroglyphic writing) inside pharaohs' tombs, and Europeans were scratching weird marks onto pieces of rock, the Khoisan of South Africa were painting their walls with beautiful, multi-colored wildlife.

The pyramids were gigantic tombstones. Inside were spaces for dead pharaohs, mummified for heaven.

Six million tons of stone were hauled 500 miles to build the largest pyramid. The blocks were piled up amazingly neatly – only 0.009% out of line.

After 3,000 years, the Egyptian civilization finally collapsed after Queen Cleopatra was bitten by a snake in 30 B.C. (*below right*).

PHARAOH WAZ ERE

The Egyptians were a miserable lot. Their rulers (pharaohs) spent most of their lives preparing for death. People believed that when they died, they either went to a five-star luxury heaven or were chewed up by a horrible half-hippo, half-crocodile monster (*right*).

In the meantime, the Egyptians had made some useful discoveries, such as counting in tens (i.e. on their fingers) and a year of 365 1/4 days. Another plus point was the position of women. The oldest Egyptian deity was the goddess Isis, and women could rule – if they wore fake beards like Hatshepsut (1473–1458 B.C.).

MAKING CHINA

Chinese history divides into dynasties named after ruling families. The word "China" comes from the Ch'in Dynasty (spelled Qin but pronounced "Chin," so the country ought to be Qina). As in Mesopotamia, Chinese super-brainy people set up a waterworks civilization (2200 B.C.). Its center was the Yellow River.

Chinese historians invented the Xia Dynasty, since there was no dynasty when civilization began. Xia ruler no.1 was Tu, a mythical canal manager.

The Chinese moved from agriculture to irrigation, plows, towns, pottery, metalworking, writing, and the worship of gods and goddesses.

The Chinese thought up most of these things themselves and made some (like cast iron), long before anyone else.

The Shang were the first royal family (about 1700–1100 B.C.). But China's royals didn't amount to much until the Qin Dynasty set up the Chinese Empire in 221 B.C.

The Chinese saw outsiders as "barbarians" and built a great wall to keep them out. Behind the wall, the emperor lounged around in his palace and left the running of the country to servants clever enough to pass exams (*top*).

There was no official religion but most Chinese respected the teachings of the wise man Confucius (page 32).

When many things went wrong at the same time, the ruling dynasty was thought to have lost "heaven's approval" and was rejected by the gods (*right*). Thus the Qin Dynasty was replaced by the Han, Jin, and Sui. Although dynasties came and went, Chinese culture went on forever.

GHOSTLY PALS

Shang kings didn't mind dying, but hated the thought of loneliness. When one of them died, his servants and animals were shoved into his tomb with him – to keep him company in the world to come.

To make sure the servants reached the afterlife, they were beheaded before burial.

The Great Wall
of China

CASTE MASTERS

Indus River

Harappa

The fourth great waterworks civilization began beside the Indus River, hence "India." By 3000 B.C., Indian farmers had potters' wheels and copper goods. Then, possibly after borrowing some Sumerian ideas, they leaped into civilization.

The Indus civilization rested on canals and bricks. It is known as Harappan, after the huge brick city at Harappa.

Harappans had houses with bathrooms (*top*) and drains, cotton clothes, an unreadable picture writing, and regular weights and measures.

This was a false start. In about 1700 B.C. the Harappans vanished mysteriously – perhaps flooded out? Wild Aryan people invaded and took years to get the civilization habit.

When the light of history came on again, it showed a Hindu civilization around the Ganges River (600 B.C.). People were arranged in four *castes* (or groups): priests, merchants, soldiers, and everyone else.

PEACE MAN
Horrified by the blood of battle, the Mauryan King Asoka became a Buddhist (about 250 B.C.). He said everyone was his child (not literally) and carved a kindly Universal Law for them on pillars.
He set up conveniences, too, such as hotels and shady trees for travelers.

Hindu culture was set out in holy books (*Veda*) and two great epic stories, the *Ramayana* and *Mahabharata*. Nobleman Siddhartha Gautama found peace under a bodhi tree and founded Buddhism (528 B.C.).

In the 4th century B.C., a fan of Alexander the Great (page 30) named Chandaragupta (not to be confused with Chandara Gupta) founded the Mauryan Empire. When it was up and running, he starved himself to death.

After another miserable period, Chandara Gupta (not to be confused with Chandaragupta!) set up the Gupta Empire (380 B.C.), which became the envy of Asia.

Ganges River

Roamin' Troops
The trade between Gupta and Roman Empires meant that some South Indian kings had Roman bodyguards!

Caste Out
Over 3,000 years, the original four castes became 3,000.

Members of different castes were not allowed to have anything to do with each other.

BASHERS AND KNOCKERS

Since the *Homo* tribe began in Africa, it is odd that those still living there didn't make more of the place.

The reason was climate. As the world grew hotter, a curtain of jungle and desert cut the south of the continent off from the rest of the world (*left*). But, civilization continued in the north.

Around 1000 B.C., the Sudanese Kushites established the first African kingdom outside Egypt.

They once occupied Egypt but were driven out by Assyrians. The Kushites then settled down around the city of Meroe (650 B.C.) where they created their own kind of Egyptian civilization with pyramids (*left*) and an even more complex system of hieroglyphics.

Let's Rock
The Askumites of Ethiopia carved a church from solid rock.

By 325 A.D., the Kushites were overrun by the Askumites of Ethiopia. They were great traders, carvers, and diggers. The rest of Africa was rather empty. Because the few people who lived there didn't write or build much, it is difficult to figure out what they did all day. But they were great artists.

The Nigerian Nok farmers and miners created lovely sculptures (500 B.C.–300 A.D.). Meanwhile, further south, Khoisan artists decorated their caves with brilliant animals (*below*).

THE TRIBE-BASHER
Imperator Caesar Lucius Septimus Severus Pertinax (Severus for short) was the greatest African of his day. Born in Libya, Severus became a star soldier. In 193 A.D., when the position of Roman emperor was up for grabs, Severus' soldiers believed he was just the man for the job.

He duly marched to Italy, became emperor, rebuilt Rome, beat up the crafty Parthians, and was about to do the same to the Scots when he died at York.

DOING IT THEIR WAY

Humans crossed from Asia to North America in about 30,000 B.C. Sixteen thousand years later they reached Peru. By now the road to Asia was flooded, so Americans had to fend for themselves.

The Inuits, hardy hunter-gatherers, struck north to the chilly Arctic (2000 B.C.). They stopped gathering (because there was nothing to gather) and lived as hunters. They didn't build canals and pyramids, but they came up with a very useful small boat – the kayak (*top*).

Various tribes learned to farm in what is now the southern United States. The Adenans buried their dead with bracelets and tobacco pipes (500 B.C.). The Mogollons (100 B.C.) were potaholics (*above*).

In about 1200 B.C., the Olmec civilization sprang up in Central America. It soon had towns, weaving, organized religion, art, grand buildings, picture writing, and a calendar.

In many ways the maize-munching Olmecs lived like their relatives in Asia's fertile boomerang (page 14), although they were less skilled in waterworks and didn't know about wheels.

GRINNING GOD

Pilgrims visiting Chavin de Huantar zeroed in on the huge temple, built in about 900 B.C. They climbed stairs and ramps, passed through passages and rooms until they finally came to the holy space. In the middle was a massive stone sculpture with a human body and the head of a cat. This was Lanzon, the great grinning god.

South American civilization began with the Chavins of Peru (1200–300 B.C.). Like the Egyptians, they had pyramids, mummies, and lovely art.

They also smoked dead bodies over a fire, like kippers.

MAROONED

Groups of super-brainy people wandered into south and east Asia during the low tide of the last Ice Age. The seas rose again as a result of the global warming that followed (about 10,000 B.C.). This left them cut off on various islands and peninsulas (such as Japan and Malaysia). Here they stayed, muddling about with stones and canoes, for thousands of years.

Left to their own devices, the people of the Japanese islands came up with their own culture. It is known as Jomon ("string design"), because they tied string around their unfinished pots to create patterns (11,000–300 B.C.).

Travelers came over from China in the third century B.C. and let the string people into the secrets of farming, metalwork, and potters' wheels.

Nevertheless, the Japanese did not join the advanced civilization class until after another wave of Chinese imports in the sixth century A.D.

Meanwhile, a Polynesian culture developed in Southeast Asia. By 1000 B.C. its intrepid canoeists were starting to spread their way of life around the Pacific.

MEGAMOM

Super-brainy people loved their moms. They loved them so much that their first gods were women. Most early societies worshiped a great goddess, also known as "Mother Earth" or "the Great Mother."

In Egypt, the megamom was Isis. In Japan she was Amaterasu, the sun goddess (below). Jimmu, the first emperor of Japan, said he was descended from her. Later, jealous men spread the myth that women were inferior to men, so god changed sex.

PARTY TIME

Roman silver coin 200 B.C.

The Chinese figured out how to make tough metals on their own. For years, early Americans had only soft metals like copper and silver.

The Sumerians wrote first, using toothpick-shaped scratches (called cuneiform). By 1000 B.C., the number of scratches was boiled down to twenty-two, giving us an "alphabet" (from *alpha, beta,* the first two letters of ancient Greek). Chinese writing was based on pictures, over 5,000 of them.

Lydian coin 547 B.C.

History is a lot like a birthday party: The best part is what you are left with afterward. The first civilizations left us brilliant presents: agriculture, pottery, woven cloth, metalwork, the wheel, writing, ships, math, and money.

The Japanese made some of the first pots, but kept the idea to themselves. Other people also learned to make pottery. Spinning and weaving also appeared in different places at different times.
But only Sumerian potters thought of spinning clay around on a wheel, so the invention spread slowly.

Metals were first used in the Middle East. Copper was replaced by tougher bronze, and in about 2500 B.C., super-strong iron weapons appeared. A thousand years later, the Hittites began driving hard bargains with soft silver coins.

Homo-something-or-other floated around on logs for thousands of years before the first ship was launched about 6500 B.C. Sails came 2,500 years later.

Chinese coin 300 B.C.

WAR, GORE, AND ARMIES

Humans – especially men – are an aggressive group. Prehistoric people fought to get the warmest cave or the biggest mammoth steak. But there weren't enough of them for battles. Besides, there were no fields to fight over and they spent most of their energy hunting and gathering.

LION KING
Like all Assyrian kings, Ashurbanipal (668–627 BC) thought he was super macho. When not slaughtering people, he killed animals as part of his religious duty. His tally: 370 lions, 250 wild oxen, and 30 elephants – what a liar!

Civilization changed all this. As well as plows and pyramids, it brought war, gore, and armies. The Egyptians were fighting each other by 3100 B.C. After that, hardly a year passed without someone going to war.

This did not stop civilization from spreading, particularly around the Middle East. The Hittites, ruled by tongue-twister kings like Hattushili and Suppululiumas, set up an empire in Turkey (2000–1200 B.C.). When this fizzled out, the blood-thirsty Assyrians (*right*) took over as the region's top power.

Horse Play
The ancient city of Troy really did exist (3000–1200 B.C.), but probably not the wooden horse.

Further south, the Hebrews clung to their piece of land around Jerusalem (*right*). Nearby, the Phoenicians of Tyre and Sidon grew fat on the profits of trade (1500–700 B.C.).

Meanwhile, two M civilizations were making names for themselves. M1 was the Minoan civilization on the isle of Crete, famous for its palaces, pottery, and holy bulls. M2 was Mycenae, a huge fortress city on the Greek mainland (1600–1120 B.C.).

About 1475 B.C., Crete was smashed up by an earthquake. The Mycenaens took over the island and its trade for 300 years, until the whole M-world mysteriously fell apart.

Rough Riders
Young Minoans played bull jumping – the craziest sport of all time (left).

LEFT OUT IN THE COLD

The wind of civilization blew across Europe from southeast to the northwest at about one mile a year. For example, farming left the south of France in about 5000 B.C. and reached Britain in 4000 B.C.

Metalworking moved a bit quicker, making the trip from Crete to Scotland in 1,000 years. While Minoan kings were sipping wine with their feet up in warm, clean palaces, Scottish chiefs were shivering in drafty huts littered with bones and animal droppings (*right*).

At Skara Brae on the Isle of Orkney in Scotland, however, there is a Stone Age village (about 3000 B.C.). It is complete with stone walls, stone floors, stone knives, stone cupboards, stone beds, etc.

MEANWHILE ...
While the Egyptians were piling up lumps of stone to make pyramids (about 2500 B.C.), the people of Northwest Europe were laying out their stones in neat patterns on the ground.

Some stood in rows (e.g. Carnac, France), others were laid out in circles (e.g. Avebury, England). Occasionally, they were balanced on top of each other, as at Stonehenge, England.

Designer Rocks
Stonehenge was probably a mix of a temple and a gigantic sundial.

In the sixth century B.C., the Celts came trampling across Northwest Europe. They were a drunken, fiery-tempered, creative farming people with names often ending in "-ix." They lived in tribes and built huge hill-forts. As well as reckless chariot drivers, they were superb craft workers in metal, glass, and enamel.

Celt Kits
The Celts cheered themselves up by wearing bright woolly clothes.

The early Europeans had no writing, although they did carve strange cup-and-ring shapes on rocks (3000 B.C.). Normally, only their pots (or pieces of pot) and arrangements of stones have survived.

LEAGUE LEADERS

By 500 B.C., two teams headed the "Euro-Near-Eastern Civilization League (E.N.E.C.L.):" King Darius' Persia on the right and king-free Greece on the left.

In the 490 B.C. play-off Darius invaded Greece and was defeated at the Battle of Marathon. This saved Greek civilization and inspired Greece's fans to take up long-distance running (*above*).

The ancient Greeks were civilization's litterbugs: Everyone following them found something Greek to pick up. Greeks lived in independent cities. The two most famous were Athens (the brains) and Sparta (the brawn). There were Greek-style cities all over the Mediterranean, too. Alexander the Great (336–323 B.C. *above*) used fire and the sword to spread the Greek lifestyle as far as India.

Slavery was one of the Greek's nastier habits. But because slaves did all the boring jobs, the Greeks had time to laze about in steamy baths and think like no one had ever thought before. They were brilliant at math, finding answers to complicated problems about triangles, squares, etc. (*below*). They invented theaters and plays, and even figured out why bath water rose when they got in!

BODY LANGUAGE
The Greeks loved their bodies. They steamed them, scrubbed them, scraped them, sculpted them, oiled them, and exercised them. They even invented the Olympic Games (776 B.C.) to show them off – every tiny bit of them!

People Power
The Athenians thought up a great new type of government, called democracy (about 508 B.C.). The idea was simple: The government should look after all citizens, so all citizens should have a say in the government. The system worked well until Rome won the "E.N.E.C.L." in 146 B.C. (below). After this, kings, queens, dictators, etc. hid democracy away for centuries.

THE DOERS

Celts
Rome
Greece

Before about 500 B.C., Europe was a hodge podge of semibarbaric tribes (north) and civilized trading cities (south). Latin-speaking Romans joined most of them together.

If the Greeks were thinkers, the Romans were doers. They defeated their scatter-brained neighbors with well-ordered armies, then sent in officials to set up the Roman way of life.

Once the conquered people were organized, they joined the Roman army and the process began all over again.

THAT CAESAR GEEZER

Julius Caesar was the Roman superstar. Make a speech? No problem. He was the best public speaker of his day. Write a best-seller? Sure. His Commentaries *are still read today. Take over France? He came, saw, and conquered the whole place. Become part of the language? Julius Caesar lives on in the words* July *and* Czar *(emperor). His enemies assassinated him in 44 B.C. because they believed he was getting too big for his boots. Surprise, surprise!*

Starting from Rome (founded 753 B.C.), the Romans first took over the rest of Italy. Next came Greece and Spain, followed by Egypt, the Balkans, and parts of Turkey. By 117 A.D. a band of Roman law and order stretched from northern England to Babylon.

Life in the Roman Empire was pretty good (unless you were a slave, when it was usually utter misery). Roads and officials were straight; public baths and entertainment were hot (*right*); buildings and security were impressive. The only real problems were at the top.

After doing away with kings, for years Rome was run by its citizens. In 27 B.C. they let Augustus become emperor. This was fine while he lived, but he was followed by some of the most revolting weirdos ever to slip into a toga.

Pony Power
Crazy Emperor Caligula (37–41 A.D.) made his horse a member of the Roman government.

ZAP-GODS AND HOLY MEN

As soon as people appeared on Earth, they wondered why they were there. They also wondered what made things grow, why the sun was never late, and where people went when they died. In other words, humans were religious creatures.

Early religion was like magic. Its purposes were  to make life pleasant by getting gods and goddesses on your side and to book a place somewhere nice after death.

1

Pleasing the gods and goddesses was done by worship and sacrifice. Worship meant talking to them in a respectful and well-mannered way (praying) and making flattering images of them. The Indian sun-god Surya, for example, was shown as large, plump, and healthy (*right*).

Sacrifice meant giving gods and goddesses precious gifts. Central Americans thought their sun-god was fond of blood, so they kept him shining with gory festivals.

2

Most religions believed in life after death. The Hindus of India believed everyone would be born again, even if only as an ant. Other people worshiped their ancestors, so they preserved their bodies. The Mesopotamians even pickled their dead in honey pots.

HONEY

K'UNG THE MASTER
Confucius (meaning Master K'ung) was a Chinese scholar who lived from 551–479 B.C. He taught people to live simply and do their duty.

This was not really a religion. Later, however, the Chinese were expected to make sacrifices to K'ung, as well as to heaven, Earth, dead emperors, etc.

In time, well-organized religions emerged. The Jews worshiped a single god. Other religions, like Hinduism and the Japanese Shintoism, kept faith with many gods.

The mystical religions of Buddhism and Confucianism were more interested in proper living than worship (*right*).

The first religions weren't about people being nice to each other. In fact, early worship often required really bizarre rituals, such as cutting out hearts to feed blood to the sun-god (*page 32*).

Many gods and goddesses didn't set an example of good behavior, either.
Zeus, the king of the ancient Greek gods (*above*), zapped those he didn't like with thunderbolts. Gods like Zeus were just superhumans, worshiped because they scared the living daylights out of people.

Some civilized people began to have doubts about such zap-gods.
Eastern holy men (e.g. Confucius and Buddha) believed religion was not about side-stepping thunderbolts, but about being a decent person.
Several Greek thinkers agreed with them. Meanwhile, the Jews had decided that there was only one, invisible, all-powerful god.

These ideas came together in the teaching of a charismatic Jewish holy man named Jesus. He said he was the son (or "Christ") of the one god who was more interested in loving than zapping.

Jesus' message became a bit muddled and mysterious because his followers, the Christians, didn't write it down until years after his death.

CONSTANTINE I
The Roman emperor Constantine I (306-337 A.D.) made Christianity the official religion of his empire.
There is a story that he became a Christian because he felt guilty that his wife Fausta boiled herself to death in her bath.

None of this stopped the new religion Christianity from becoming incredibly popular. It quickly spread from Palestine throughout the Roman Empire, then seeped down into Africa and to the East.

Double Act
By 400 A.D., statues of Jesus and his mother filled churches all over Europe. By 540, cathedrals like Constantinople's St. Sophia (above) were also being built.

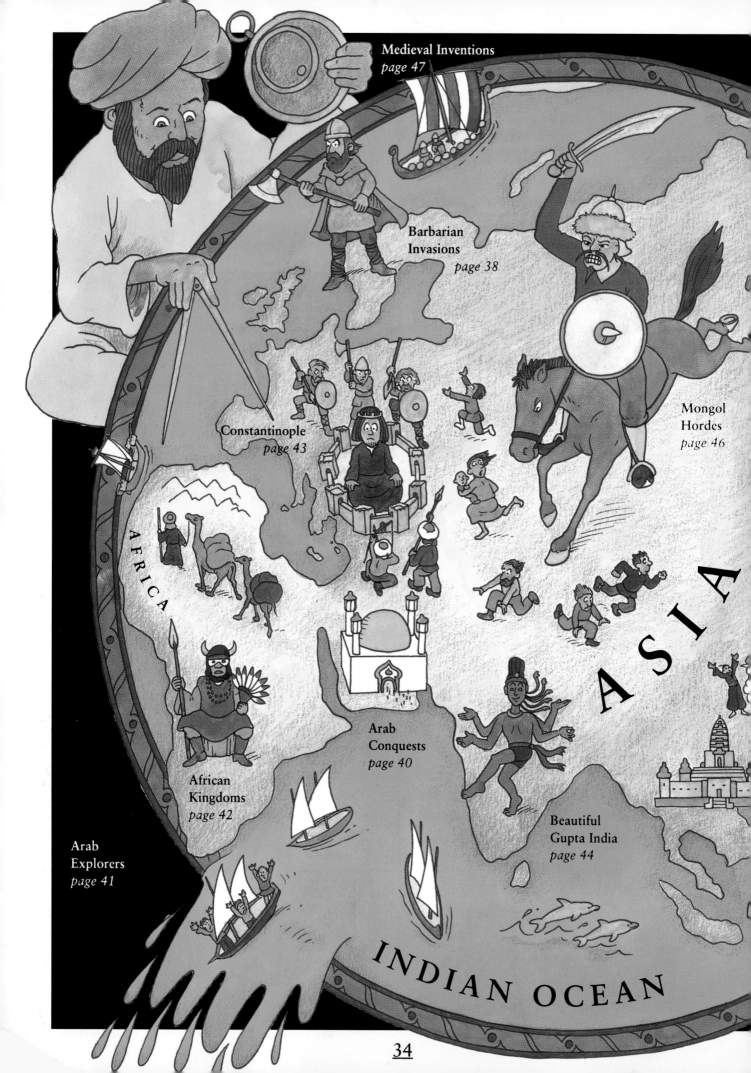

Medieval Inventions
page 47

Barbarian
Invasions
page 38

Mongol
Hordes
page 46

Constantinople
page 43

AFRICA

ASIA

African
Kingdoms
page 42

Arab
Conquests
page 40

Beautiful
Gupta India
page 44

Arab
Explorers
page 41

INDIAN OCEAN

3 AND THEN...

HALF TIME

Easter Island
page 48

Japanese Samurais
page 49

Mayan Pyramids
page 50

Tang Dynasty Fireworks
page 45

Crusaders
page 41

P A C I F I C   O C E A N

The world got a bit chillier in the first few centuries A.D. Less food grew; people became hungry and quarrelsome; countless starving warriors galloped out of central Asia, bumping into other tribes and jumbling up the civilization jigsaw. In China the heavens stopped approving of the Han Dynasty (page 45) but couldn't find anyone to take its place. The Roman Empire split into half-Roman and half-Greek. Then the Roman half broke into lots of smaller pieces.

Troublesome groups continued to pour out of Asia for another 1,000 years. When the last horrible horde (the Mongols) finally dismounted and came indoors, Asia, Europe, and North Africa sighed with relief.

Civilization had taken quite a bashing. Apart from Islam and windmills, there hadn't been many new ideas. Just staying alive and more or less civilized had been enough for most people. Only pilgrims and Arab traders had traveled very far.

The Americans and people of the Pacific still thought the world was all theirs. Europeans and Middle Easterners took an occasional swipe at each other. Southern Africans remained behind their curtain and the Chinese hid behind their wall. Compared with what had gone before and what came after, it was all a bit disappointing.

500 A.D. TO 1350 A.D.

	400	500	600	700	800	900

AFRICA

400 Christianity spreads in Aksumite Empire of Ethiopia.

500–1100 Ghana, ruled by the Goldmasters, at its peak in West Africa.

632–750 Muslim Arabs expand across North Africa.

800 Arabs and Persians found trading stations along the east African coast.

EUROPE

432 St. Patrick brings Christianity to Ireland.

445 Attila the Hun attacks Western Europe.

449 Angles, Saxons, and Jutes begin conquest of Britain.

527–65 Reign of Byzantine Emperor Justinian, who tries and fails to unite the Eastern (Ottoman) and Western (Catholic) Christian churches.

476 Last Roman emperor in West is deposed.

602 Slavs begin to settle in the Balkans.

680 Bulgars invade Balkans.

610–41 Emperor Heraclius begins Byzantine Empire.

732 Battle of Poitiers halts Arab expansion into Western Europe.

711 Muslim invasion of Spain.

809–17 War between Byzantine Empire and Bulgars.

843 Frankish Empire breaks up.

787 Viking raids begin.

800 First castles built in Western Europe.

800 Frankish king Charlemagne crowned Holy Roman Emperor.

AMERICA

400 Zapotec state flourishes in southern Mexico.

500 Hopewell culture makes pottery and uses iron weapons.

600 Huari (Peru) and Tiahuanaco (Bolivia) Empires flourish.

700 Maya civilization at its peak in Southern Mexico.

ASIA

531 Chosroes I comes to throne. Sassanian Empire at its greatest.

500 Polynesians settle in Hawaiian Islands and Easter Island.

467 Gupta Empire destroyed by the Huns.

550 Buddhism introduced into Japan.

625 Muhammad begins his mission to spread Islam.

618–907 China under Tang Dynasty.

646 Political and social reforms in Japan. Japan copies Chinese government.

645 Buddism reaches Tibet.

632–641 Arabs conquer Syria, Persia, Egypt, and parts of North Africa.

605–610 Sui build grand canal linking Yangtze to captial at Chang'an.

589 China reunited by Wen di, who begins Sui Dynasty.

700 Easter islanders begin to build stone platforms.

730 Printing in China.

760 Arabs adopt Indian numerals and develop algebra and trigonometry.

750 Abbasid Caliphate set up (Persia).

751 Papermaking spreads to Muslim world and Europe.

811 House of Wisdom set up in Baghdad.

850s Arabs perfect astrolab[e]

802 Jayavarman II set up Khmer Kingdom in Cambodia.

886–1267 Chola Dynas[ty] rules in Sout[h] India.

858 Fujiwara domination of Japanese emperors begins

868 First book printed in China.

36

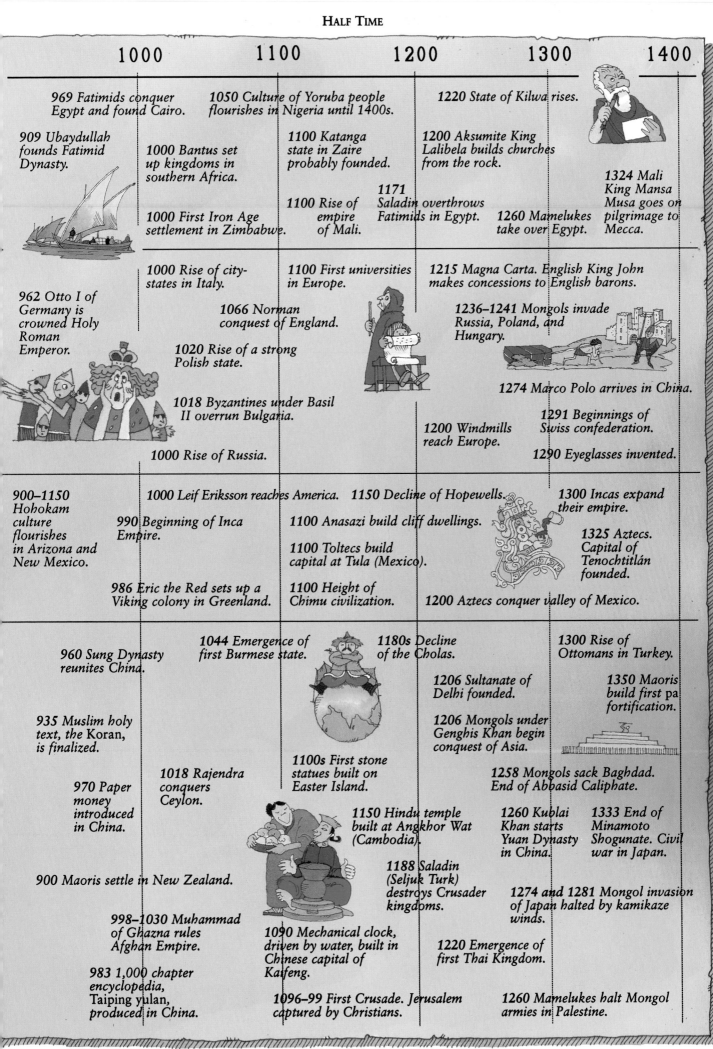

1000 · 1100 · 1200 · 1300 · 1400

969 Fatimids conquer Egypt and found Cairo.

909 Ubaydullah founds Fatimid Dynasty.

1000 Bantus set up kingdoms in southern Africa.

1000 First Iron Age settlement in Zimbabwe.

1050 Culture of Yoruba people flourishes in Nigeria until 1400s.

1100 Katanga state in Zaire probably founded.

1100 Rise of empire of Mali.

1171 Saladin overthrows Fatimids in Egypt.

1220 State of Kilwa rises.

1200 Aksumite King Lalibela builds churches from the rock.

1260 Mamelukes take over Egypt.

1324 Mali King Mansa Musa goes on pilgrimage to Mecca.

962 Otto I of Germany is crowned Holy Roman Emperor.

1000 Rise of city-states in Italy.

1066 Norman conquest of England.

1020 Rise of a strong Polish state.

1018 Byzantines under Basil II overrun Bulgaria.

1000 Rise of Russia.

1100 First universities in Europe.

1215 Magna Carta. English King John makes concessions to English barons.

1236–1241 Mongols invade Russia, Poland, and Hungary.

1274 Marco Polo arrives in China.

1200 Windmills reach Europe.

1291 Beginnings of Swiss confederation.

1290 Eyeglasses invented.

900–1150 Hohokam culture flourishes in Arizona and New Mexico.

990 Beginning of Inca Empire.

986 Eric the Red sets up a Viking colony in Greenland.

1000 Leif Eriksson reaches America.

1100 Anasazi build cliff dwellings.

1100 Toltecs build capital at Tula (Mexico).

1100 Height of Chimu civilization.

1150 Decline of Hopewells.

1200 Aztecs conquer valley of Mexico.

1300 Incas expand their empire.

1325 Aztecs. Capital of Tenochtitlán founded.

960 Sung Dynasty reunites China.

935 Muslim holy text, the Koran, is finalized.

970 Paper money introduced in China.

900 Maoris settle in New Zealand.

998–1030 Muhammad of Ghazna rules Afghan Empire.

983 1,000 chapter encyclopedia, Taiping yulan, produced in China.

1044 Emergence of first Burmese state.

1018 Rajendra conquers Ceylon.

1100s First stone statues built on Easter Island.

1090 Mechanical clock, driven by water, built in Chinese capital of Kaifeng.

1096–99 First Crusade. Jerusalem captured by Christians.

1180s Decline of the Cholas.

1206 Sultanate of Delhi founded.

1206 Mongols under Genghis Khan begin conquest of Asia.

1150 Hindu temple built at Angkhor Wat (Cambodia).

1188 Saladin (Seljuk Turk) destroys Crusader kingdoms.

1220 Emergence of first Thai Kingdom.

1300 Rise of Ottomans in Turkey.

1350 Maoris build first pa fortification.

1258 Mongols sack Baghdad. End of Abbasid Caliphate.

1260 Kublai Khan starts Yuan Dynasty in China.

1333 End of Minamoto Shogunate. Civil war in Japan.

1274 and 1281 Mongol invasion of Japan halted by kamikaze winds.

1260 Mamelukes halt Mongol armies in Palestine.

THE GREAT PUSHOVER

The Roman Empire didn't fall, it was pushed. What's more, this happened because it was nice, not nasty. For hundreds of years wild people had peered in from outside, longing to try on a toga, take a bath, etc.

So when the Romans dropped their guard, in poured Huns and Alans, Slavs and Avars, Vandals, Picts, and an assortment of Goths (who sacked Rome in 410 A.D.).

These barbarians didn't have a clue how to run the place. Soon togas needed mending, the bath water ran cold, and the empire went down the drain. In its place was a motley collection of mini-kingdoms, ruled by boozing, hard-hatted hoodlums whose idea of civilization was a good sack.

In some places, helped by fire and sword, the mini-kingdoms joined together. No one did this better than Charlemagne (*right*), a 9th-century king of the Franks (i.e., France). His kingdom was so huge that it looked like the Roman Empire. Charlemagne even called himself Holy Roman Emperor (in 800).

It was all too good to last. Charlemagne's empire fell apart and plundering Vikings (*left*) sailed down from the north with fresh fire and sword (787–1066). For a while it looked as if Christendom (Christian Europe) was going back to square one.

THE SCHOLAR AND THE SLAVEGIRL

Safe in his Jarrow monastery (England), the Venerable Bede (born 673) wrote hymns, textbooks, and a really useful history. Further south, St. Bathild (born 630) was captured by pirates and sold into slavery. Luckily, she married a king and spent the rest of her life urging people to pray, stop slavery, wash, etc. In such ways women and monks kept civilization going.

By about 1300, some parts of Christendom were quite pleasant to live in again. Towns such as Paris, London, and (especially) Venice were large and bustling with trade. There were some reasonably fair laws and courts. A few boys went to school (*below*). One or two buildings (mostly cathedrals) were worth looking at.

Some places, such as England and France, were quite well run. It didn't compare with China or the Muslim world, but it was a start.

Germany and Italy were made up of lots of small states, cities, etc. Elsewhere there were countries, such as Denmark, Scotland, and Hungary. Further east, the Rus, a Viking people, carved out a place of their own (Russia), complete with Byzantine-style Christianity (page 43).

The first great Rus king, Vladimir I (978–1015), became Christian because other faiths wouldn't let him drink (*right*).

It took a lot of Christian puff to get rid of the dark clouds of barbarism (*above*). Priests, monks, nuns, bishops, archbishops, and others blew more or less together, conducted by the pope (the church's leader).

The Christian Saint
"Good king" Wenceslas was in fact a duke, but he was good. The Christian saint was murdered by his beastly pagan brother, Boleslav, in 936.

Some kings had lots of Christian puff (e.g. the Czech Good King Wenceslas), others were just a nuisance (e.g. King Louis Lazybones of France).

POT LUCK – THE FEUDAL SYSTEM
Medieval kings gave their followers (lords) land. In return, lords fought for the king or gave him money. The lords handed out land to their followers. This went on down to the peasants. They were so poor that all they could give their lords were a few cabbages or the contents of their chamber pots (useful fertilizer).

THE SUPER SHISH KEBAB

Because Arabia is a rather dry, boring place, for the first few thousand years of civilization not much happened there. Then came Muhammad the Muslim, the last great holy man.

Taking a nap in a cave near Mecca (left-hand edge of Arabia), Muhammad (570–632 A.D.) found himself tuned into the word of the Supreme Being Allah. Amazed, he told his Arab friends. They agreed it was absolutely brilliant and set off on their camels to tell everyone else.

The Muslim Arabs got so carried away with surrendering to Allah (Islam) they made everyone surrender to them. They conquered a huge empire in no time at all (632–750, *below*).

As empires go, the Arab Empire was easy-going. The Arabs were happy to leave most people alone – as long as they paid their taxes. Their empire stretched halfway around the world, from Spain to the borders of China. Its rulers were *caliphs*. This meant "those who take over," because they had taken over from Muhammad. The Shiites ("followers") said caliphs had to be related to Muhammad. They battled with the Sunnis ("business as usual"), who said the job was open to any Muslim. After a couple of centuries at the top, the Abbasid Empire began to break up.

ROCK BAND
The Muslims of North Africa itched to get rich in Spain. In 711, led by ex-slave Tariq, they crossed the Mediterranean, hammered the Spanish King Roderick, and pinched his kingdom. The place where they landed is "Tariq's Rock" – Jebel Tariq, or Gibraltar.

Ali the Zanj's black slave revolt almost captured Baghdad (*above*). But just when things were starting to look grim, the Abbasids found some new and rather useful friends. These were the Turks, central Asian heavies who had become Muslim.

In 1070, fighting for the Abbasid caliph, the Turks captured Jerusalem from the Egyptians. They went on to bash the living daylights out of the Byzantine emperor (page 43). Terrified, he called for help from the Christians of Western Europe. This set off 200 years of Crusades, when armor-plated Christian Europeans tried (unsuccessfully) to drive the Turks back from where they had come.

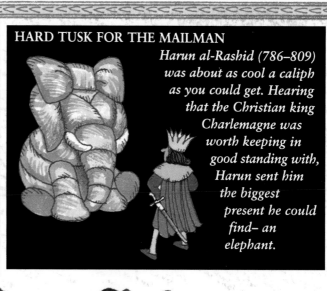

HARD TUSK FOR THE MAILMAN
Harun al-Rashid (786–809) was about as cool a caliph as you could get. Hearing that the Christian king Charlemagne was worth keeping in good standing with, Harun sent him the biggest present he could find– an elephant.

Islam turned out to be more than just a religion – it was a whole new civilization. As the Koran (the Muslims' holy book) was written in Arabic, the Arabic language spread all over the place. But Arab scholars were not bigheaded. They

respected other ideas. They added a pinch of Greek, a slice of Hindu, and twist of Christianity to Islam, and made a really exciting cultural shish kebab (*above*).

What a Racquet
Crusaders learned tennis from the Arabs in the 12th century.

At the time of the Muslim Abbasid caliphs, Baghdad (750–1258) was a brilliant city. Its House of Wisdom bulged with brains, its merchants jingled with cash, its buildings gleamed with artwork (*right*).

Arab scientists invented the astrolabe, a finger-pinching instrument for finding the position of ships at sea (*below*). They designed the system of numbers we use and figured out fractions. Finally, they were probably the first people to realize that nothing is zero and vice versa.

AND THEN...A HISTORY OF THE WORLD

CULTURE CAKE

The Arabs took all of Africa above the Sahara sand curtain into their Islamic empire.

However, the tough Berbers of North Africa welcomed Islam but not the Arabs. In 909, Berber leader Ubaydullah finally washed the Sunni Arabs out of his people's hair and set up the Fatimid Empire. Ubaydullah claimed he was descended from Muhammad's daughter Fatima (making him a Shiite).

It's hard to see behind the Sahara sand curtain. The Bantu of Southern Africa bumbled around with cattle, pottery, and the usual Stone Age accessories. Arab traders, always on the lookout for a quick buck, set up depots on the East African coast (*above*). Inland lay the mysterious K-kingdoms of Katanga (Zaire) and Kilwa (Tanzania).

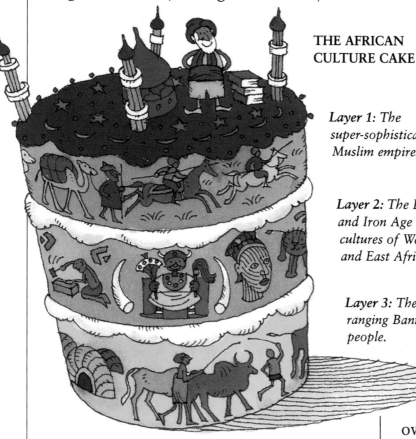

THE AFRICAN CULTURE CAKE

Layer 1: The super-sophisticated Muslim empires.

Layer 2: The Bronze and Iron Age cultures of West and East Africa.

Layer 3: The cattle-ranging Bantu bush people.

As long as they kept out of the way of the Berbers, the West Africans did rather better.

Ruled by its *Kaya Maghan* ("Goldmasters"), Ghana made a fortune selling slaves, salt, and gold dust (*above*). When Mali took over as the region's no. 1 power, its king was said to be rich enough to afford 10,000 horses for his stables. By the 11th century, it also boasted a sort of university in Timbuktu.

The Fatimid Empire lasted about 100 years, before it fell to a Berber revolt. Further east, the Christian Aksumites fled into the mountains to escape the Muslims. They were the only non-Muslim Africans able to write, but couldn't even get a postcard through to fellow Christians to say how they were (*left*). Later they reappeared as Ethiopians (page 69).

ROME AGAIN

Before the Roman Empire was "Vandalized," Emperor Constantine gave it a new headquarters. He found a nice little plot – Byzantium – in Turkey, but didn't like the name. "Rome II" sounded too ordinary, so he chose "Constantinople," so he would never be forgotten (330 A.D.).

The citizens of Constantinople were Greek-speaking. They were known as Romans or Byzantines because "Constantinoplians" was a bit of a mouthful. Cleverly located on the east-west, north-south crossroads, their city became the biggest, richest, and craziest in the world.

The Byzantine emperors took over the remains of the old Roman Empire. They had their own, pope-less (Orthodox) type of Christianity. Roman Catholic priests shaved but did not marry; Orthodox priests did the opposite.

Byzantine bezants were a magnet for invaders. First came the Sassanids, who had taken over and redesigned the Persian Empire. No sooner had Heraclius the Hero (610–641) beaten them off, than Arab camels came thundering over the horizon.

BASHER'S BLIND DATE
In 1014, Byzantine emperor Basil II – "The Basher of Bulgars" – smashed the Bulgars at the Battle of Belasica.
He divided his prisoners into 100 groups of 100, blinded 9,900 of them, and told the others (left with one eye) to lead their friends home. When the grisly procession reached the Bulgar leader Czar Samuel, he died of shock.

Visitors to Constantinople sighed at the size of its Sophia Church (see page 33), marveled at its mosaics, wondered at its walls, and banked its bezants (gold coins).

Bits and Pieces
Byzantine artists decorated their churches with marvelous mosaics.

The Arabs stole most of the Byzantine Empire for Islam but couldn't get through Constantinople's amazing walls (*above*). Nor could the Bulgars, nor could the Turks (not until 1453, anyway).

Sulking Sassanids
The Sassanids (225–651) often defeated the Byzantines, but never quite captured Constantinople.

BELLYBUTTONS AND SALESMEN

काका वृश
बसतः द्वा
न समर्गंत

Gupta India was some place (320–467 A.D.) – beautiful Greek-style buildings, decorated with curvy pictures and carvings; Buddhism blossomed; the Hindu religion, with its fixed caste system, grew deeper roots; Kalidasa and others wrote lovely poems etc. in the Sanskrit language (*above*).

Sadly, Gupta greatness came to a sticky end in 467. A Hun-like people invaded from the north, and, for the next 700 years, India's civilization was found in separate states rather than one large one. There was occasional trouble from traveling Muslim salesmen (e.g. Arabs in 712). In time, however, most of them married local women and settled down as honorary Indians.

MEANWHILE
While Indians worshiped in temples filled with dancing girls and statues dressed in beaded beach-clothes (or less), even a hint of bare flesh filled the priests of Christian Europe with horror (and secret wishes).

Meanwhile, southern India was in quite a "palaver." The ruling dynasty – Pallava – built splendid towns (usually called puram). Mamallapuram and Kanchipuram were decorated with fantastic ornamental temples.

When the Cholas took over (about 886), the Hindu civilization became even more powerful. The repeater king Rajaraja I (985–1014) and his son Rajendra I took over Ceylon and sent great fleets to the east (*top*).

In the late 12th century, the Turks burst into India. The latest Islamic salesmen, they beat up the Hindus and Buddhists and made a Muslim state, based on Delhi. Its first sultan was an ex-slave, Izz Ad-Din Abu Al-Mansur Aybak. He refused to become an honorary Indian.

Mosque Makers
The Muslim conquerors of India demolished Hindu temples and used the stone to build shiny new mosques.

TANG TIME

In 220 A.D., the Chinese Han Dynasty lost Heaven's permission to rule. After 370 years of woe, Emperor Wen di (Sui Dynasty) led China out of the Never-Never Land of civil war (*above*). The Sui got zillions of people to build a canal joining the Yellow and Yangtze Rivers, then surrendered to the Tang Dynasty.

Tang time (618–907) was the golden period of Chinese history. Artists and inventors (but not peasants) flourished and Chinese culture became all the rage in eastern Asia. But slowed by Arabs and rebellions, Tang time finally ran out and China split into 10 states.

SUPERMARKET
Everyone who was anyone came to Tang China. In the fantastic Tang capital, Ch'ang-an (population 2 million), Indians, Arabs, Persians, Byzantines, Turks, and the odd European wrangled in the world's greatest market.

Tang Bang
The Chinese probably invented gunpowder in the 8th century A.D. It should really be called firework powder, because at the time they hadn't invented guns!

In 960, the Sung swung in. Heaven let them rule until the Jurchen (or Manchu) came lurching into northern China.

The Sung hung on in the south, until the 13th century, when the Mongols stepped over the Great Wall.

In 1260, Mongol chief Kublai Khan set up the Yuan Dynasty with a new headquarters in Beijing. China had more of everything: more land, more canals, more rice, more soldiers, and more people (80 million).

China's emperors were incredibly rich and its peasants incredibly poor. No one could match its potters, painters, scholars, organizers, and writers.

Only the Chinese had paper (105 A.D.) and printed books (868 A.D.); burned coal in fires; used needles to make themselves better (acupuncture, *above*) and find their way around (the compass, 1000). They even had the best wheelbarrows.

45

THE FINAL FIRECRACKER

Like a huge Roman candle, central Asia kept throwing out unruly tribes for over a thousand years.

First came Huns and Vandals, then Turks, and finally the most ferocious of the lot – the Mongols.

The Mongols were brilliant horsemen and skilled shots with the bow and arrow. They were tough, too – Mongol warriors could live for weeks off their horses' milk and blood. But since all they did was charge aimlessly around the Asian plains, for years no one took much notice of them.

Then along came Genghis Khan. Taking over his dad's tribe at 13, he persuaded the unruly Mongols to try conquering. They loved it. By 1206, they had beaten up their neighbors and were ready to move on.

CONQUER CHAMPION
Temujin, the boy from Deligun Bulduk (to the right of the back of beyond), had a dream. He wanted to conquer the world.

After changing his name to Genghis Khan ("King of the Whole Lot"), he set out to get it. He didn't quite succeed, but when he died (1227) he had set a world conquering record that has never been broken.

The Mongols mangled China in no time. Traveling in hordes, they then zoomed across Asia to the Black Sea. They went on to crumple Russia, gallop into Europe, and flatten Baghdad. Finally, in 1260, they met the Mamelukes, Turkish ex-slaves who had recently nabbed Egypt. Determined not to lose it, the Mamelukes beat the Mongols at the Battle of Goliath Springs in Palestine. The final firecracker had burned itself out.

Route of Mongols

Mongolia

Russia

Tibet

China

Persia

India

Burma

Sia

UNDERWEAR, WIND, AND WATER

For thousands of years civilization was heaved along by slaves, peasants, and animals. But super-brainy people knew that Nature's muscles – wind and water – were far stronger. The problem was how to use them.

Wind power was first captured with sails. Next came windmills, invented in Asia and whirling around Europe by 1200. Asians also discovered that water power could turn a wheel (about 100 B.C.). One thousand years later the steady slosh-splash of the water-wheel could be heard from Beijing, China to Bristol, England. Waterwheels turned huge stones to grind corn. Later they helped do other things, such as doing the laundry.

Cobblers!
Most medieval Europeans were known by their job: Miller, Thatcher, Cooper (barrel-maker), Butcher, Brewer, Fletcher (arrow-maker), Gardener, Smith and, of course, Cobbler (shoemaker).

Telling the time was still a problem. Most people knew only Dark = Sleep and Light = Wake up. The more methodical, such as priests, tried all kinds of ways to measure hours and minutes. None of them worked very well: candle clocks blew out, hourglasses speeded up, sundials needed sunshine, water clocks dried up or froze.

STAYING ON
For staying on a horse, nothing is more useful than stirrups. They were invented in Asia and cantered west, arriving in Europe about 600 A.D.
A rider with stirrups could shoot a bow, throw a spear, or write a letter without falling off. Cavalry now jumped over infantry in importance and Europeans came up with clanking knights-in-armor.

More useful inventions included eyeglasses for seeing clearly (Italy, late 13th century), pointed rather than round arches, which allowed cathedrals to be taller and lighter than ever before, and underwear which was not only warmer but gave added safety in windy weather (*above*).

Stand Back!
The first cannons (Europe, 13th century) were often just as dangerous for those who fired them as for their targets.

PICK-AND-MIX

While the rest of the world fought, built, and invented, the Polynesians paddled. Having reached Fiji and the islands of the Central Pacific in about 1000 B.C., by 500 A.D. they had splashed over to Hawaii and Easter Island. Around 900, the Maoris doubled back and landed in New Zealand.

The Pacific people were happy fishing and chasing after moas (*left*) and dodos, so it was some time before they felt the need to build anything other than huts. In about 700, they set up some fancy stone shelves on Easter Island. By 1100, deciding they looked a bit bare, they livened them up with gigantic stone statues.

Easter Presents
The huge statues (called moai) on Easter Island may have been erected to honor stony-faced ancestors. Similar holy shapes appeared on other islands.

Back in Southeast Asia, the Polynesians' home base, the civilization habit was spreading. There was a wide range of options to choose from: Indian (Hindu or Muslim), Arab, Chinese, or a pick-and-mix culture of one's own.

In about 900, the Khmer people of Cambodia built a big stone headquarters at Ankor (*right*), complete with waterworks. Their king was a god. As being holy was more fun for him than everyone else, he let his people also take up Buddhism and Hinduism. There were other pick-and-mix civilizations (with or without running water) in Korea and Burma.

MEANWHILE...
While the Easter Islanders were heaving hard-faced statues onto empty shelves by the seashore (1100), on the other side of the world Europeans were hauling up smaller hunks of stone to raise the walls of their castles.

Because they were proud islanders, the Japanese couldn't decide whether to stick to a homemade civilization or borrow bits of China's. In 646, when the Tang were the oriental trendsetters, the Japanese chose the China option. They built a new headquarters (Nara) as a copy of Ch'ang-an and tried to organize their country Chinese-style: all pull together and do as you're told. They even got the Ainus of the north (*above*) – the original Japanese – to behave like everyone else.

BETTER LETTERS

Chinese writing (a shape for each word) was OK for the Chinese because their words were short – e.g. Tang, bin, dung, etc. It was not so useful for Japanese, which had much longer words – e.g., Yamaha, kamikaze, etc. The Japanese solved the problem by inventing letters that represented sounds (like "Ah").

Chineseification did not really work. In 858, the Fujiwara clan took over and went back to the happy-go-lucky Japanese way of doing things. The headquarters were moved from Nara to Hein-kyo. They still had an emperor, but nobody paid much attention to him.

While knights-in-armor were running Europe, knights-in-padded jackets were taking over Japan. These were the Samurai. By 1170 they had kicked out the Fujiwara and were squabbling to control the emperor. Samurai superstar Minamoto won and got the emperor to make him General No. 1 (*Sei-i tai-shogun* – or "Shogun" for short). The emperor was now a puppet, with the Shogun pulling his strings.

The Chinese objected to the Japanese doing their own un-Chinese thing. Twice (1274 and 1281) Mongol emperor Kublai Khan tried to teach his awkward neighbors a lesson. Each time his ships were blown away by holy winds (kamikaze).

Warring Samurai clans

The Shogun controls his puppet emperor

Kamikaze winds destroy the Mongol fleet of Kublai Khan

PYRAMID CRAZY

The peoples of North America were stuck on the road to civilization. They had everything they needed to go on, such as farming and waterworks, but somehow they didn't. In the north the Inuits shivered into Alaska, while tribes of hunter-gatherers ambled about the great prairies.

Further south, Mississippi peoples, such as the Hopewells (300 B.C.–700 A.D.), had iron and pots and piled up burial mounds. The Anasazi built a sideways culture on the cliffs of Arizona (1100, *left*). Not far away the Hohokam (meaning "Ho-ho You Can't Find Us") set up a great waterworks system, then vanished in 1400.

If things were quiet in the north, Central America was really buzzing. In about 300 A.D., the fantastic city of Teotihuacan sprang up in Mexico. It had bigger pyramids than Egypt, wider and longer streets than Ch'ang-an, and more people than New York City.

"TUNS" TO REMEMBER
Instead of days, months, and years, the Mayans had kins (days), uinals (20 days), tuns (360 days), katuns (7,200 days), and baktuns (144,000 days). Telephone number dates – e.g., 21/14/16/13/15 – made birthdays hard to remember and history a nightmare.

Teotihuacan's buildings gleamed with gold. Water gurgled in the fields nearby. But we haven't a clue about who lived there or where they went. (Another Ho-ho people).

Below Teotihuacan, the magnificent Mayas cleared the jungle to set up a civilization that lasted from 300 B.C. –1500 A.D. (going strong about 700).

Most Mayas were farmers, growing corn and keeping turkeys. They built grand stone cities (temples, pyramids, gold, and so on) for worship rather than to live in.

Step Aerobics
Mayan priests kept fit simply by walking up the temple steps each day.

Mayan Jam
The Mayas built sport stadiums, complete with stone rings for a game like basketball.

SNEAK PREVIEW
Sailing from Greenland in about 1000, Leif the Viking got lost. He was blown west until he bumped into a place he called Vinland. Although he didn't realize it, he was the first person to visit America since the flooding of the main Asia-America highway (page 13).

Chocaholics
The Mayas were the first people to cultivate the cacao bean – from which we get chocolate!

Mayan cities had funny names like Tikal, but the people were definitely not Ho-hos. Most of their gods, such as Kum Kax and the Jaguar, loved a drop of blood *(right)*. To fill their bloody cups, worshipers did all kinds of murderous things, such as digging holes in people. Quetzalcoatl, the feathery snake god, was about the only god who liked water with his meals; he was very popular.

South Americans carried on potting and weaving much as before. Various civilizations came and went – e.g., the Huari of Peru and the Tiahuanaco people of Bolivia (600 A.D.).

The fishing Chimu of Peru did better than most (12th century). Their headquarters at Chan Chan were larger than any European settlement and llamas clopped along a network of fine roads. As the Chan Chan gang were spreading their lifestyle northward, a new people arrived in the area.

These were the Incas. In time they chose a Sapa Inca (the One-and-Only-Inca) to lead them and started to pick up a mountain empire in the Andes. However, unknown to the Incas and Mayas (and even to Quetzalcoatl), Americans were about to get a nasty shock. Far away, European sailors were planning trips to China.

Should they sail east, or take a Leif out of the Viking book and go west?

4 AND THEN...

GETTING TO KNOW YOU

After cruising along in the slow lane for some 10,000 years, in about 1400 History put its foot down. Milestones whizzed by and the modern world, previously just a mark on the map, came into view on the horizon.

History speeded up with several important changes. Using boats to bob across the widest seas, gunslinging Europeans went traveling. Their journeys taught them what the world looked like and allowed them to introduce the various types of scattered super-brainy people to each other.

Strangers didn't always get along, of course. The European gunslingers thought they were better than everyone else. The Chinese and Japanese thought the opposite and locked the visitors out. The less confident and the gentle had to put up with a lot of unpleasant bullying.

As before – except more so – believers knocked the living daylights out of other believers, because they were different. Sometimes the differences were so small that outsiders couldn't understand what all the fuss was about.

Finally, there was a new trend in belonging. People from similar backgrounds formed themselves into countries. They became unbelievably angry if anyone suggested their country was not the best.

Explorers
page 60

Greasy Pole
page 61

Mighty Muslims
page 67

Great Zimbabwe
page 69

The Black Death
page 58

ATLANTIC OCEAN

AFRICA

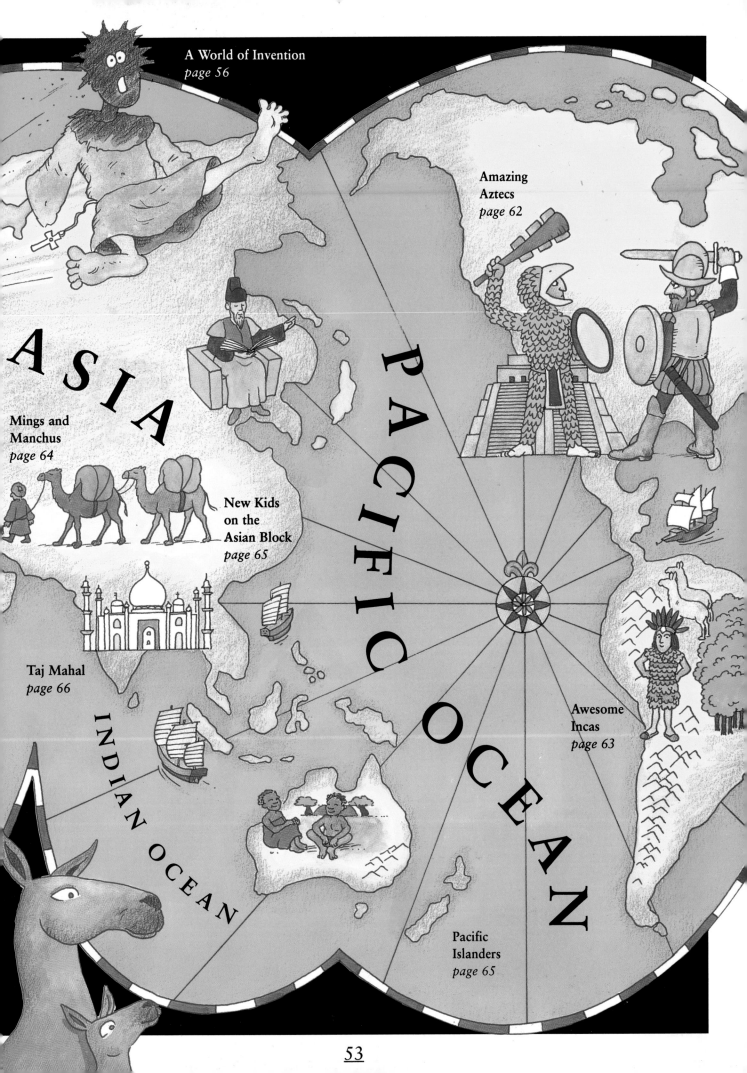

A World of Invention
page 56

Amazing
Aztecs
page 62

Mings and
Manchus
page 64

New Kids
on the
Asian Block
page 65

Taj Mahal
page 66

Awesome
Incas
page 63

Pacific
Islanders
page 65

ASIA

PACIFIC OCEAN

INDIAN OCEAN

1350 A.D. TO 1650 A.D.

1300　　　　　1400　　　　　1500

AMERICA

1450 Inca city of Machu Picchu built.

1486–1502 Aztec Empire at its height under Sapa Inca Ahuitzotl.

1492 Columbus reaches America.

1440s Under Pachacuti Inca Empire expands. Incas build great fortress at Cuzco.

1493 Treaty of Tordesillas divides New World between Portugal and Spain.

1440–1468 Reign of Aztec emperor Montezuma I. Under him, empire expands into eastern Mexico.

1493 First Spanish settlement in New World at Hispaniola.

1470 Incas conquer Chimu Kingdom.

ASIA

1405–1431 Zheng He explores Indian Ocean.

1460 Chinese porcelain exported around the world.

1341 Black Death starts in Asia.

1394 Thais invade Cambodia.

1498 Vasco da Gama reaches India.

1380 Timur Lenk begins conquests.

1501 Shah Ismail founds Safavid Dynasty in Persia.

1350 Japanese cultural revival.

1398 Timur invades India and sacks Delhi.

EUROPE

1386 Union of Poland and Lithuania.

1453 End of Hundred Years' War. England forced out of France.

1492 End of Muslim rule in Spain.

1500 Lead pencils used in England.

1337 Hundred Years' War begins between England and France (right).

1453 Ottomans capture Constantinople; end of Byzantine Empire.

1509 Watch invented.

1500s Italian Renaissance
Leonardo da Vinci (1452-1519)
Michelangelo (1475-1564)
Machiavelli (1469-1527)

1348–1352 Black Death kills one third of Europe's population.

1445 Johannes Gutenberg prints first book in Europe.

AFRICA

1462–1492 Sonni Ali ruler of the Songhai Empire.

1500s Songhai Empire at its peak under Muhammad Turré.

1492 Spanish begin conquest of North African coast.

1430 Construction of great stone enclosure at Zimbabwe (left).

1505 Portuguese develop trading posts in East Africa.

1550　　　　　　1600　　　　　　1650

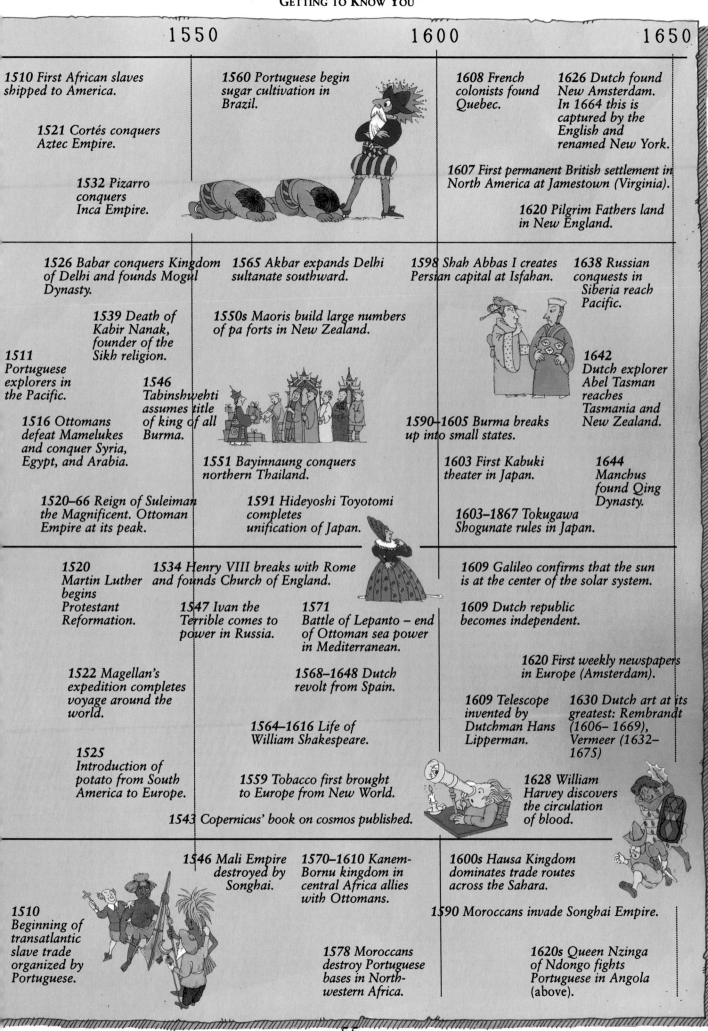

1510 First African slaves shipped to America.

1521 Cortés conquers Aztec Empire.

1532 Pizarro conquers Inca Empire.

1560 Portuguese begin sugar cultivation in Brazil.

1608 French colonists found Quebec.

1626 Dutch found New Amsterdam. In 1664 this is captured by the English and renamed New York.

1607 First permanent British settlement in North America at Jamestown (Virginia).

1620 Pilgrim Fathers land in New England.

1526 Babar conquers Kingdom of Delhi and founds Mogul Dynasty.

1539 Death of Kabir Nanak, founder of the Sikh religion.

1511 Portuguese explorers in the Pacific.

1516 Ottomans defeat Mamelukes and conquer Syria, Egypt, and Arabia.

1546 Tabinshwehti assumes title of king of all Burma.

1520–66 Reign of Suleiman the Magnificent. Ottoman Empire at its peak.

1565 Akbar expands Delhi sultanate southward.

1550s Maoris build large numbers of pa forts in New Zealand.

1551 Bayinnaung conquers northern Thailand.

1591 Hideyoshi Toyotomi completes unification of Japan.

1598 Shah Abbas I creates Persian capital at Isfahan.

1590–1605 Burma breaks up into small states.

1603 First Kabuki theater in Japan.

1603–1867 Tokugawa Shogunate rules in Japan.

1638 Russian conquests in Siberia reach Pacific.

1642 Dutch explorer Abel Tasman reaches Tasmania and New Zealand.

1644 Manchus found Qing Dynasty.

1520 Martin Luther begins Protestant Reformation.

1522 Magellan's expedition completes voyage around the world.

1525 Introduction of potato from South America to Europe.

1534 Henry VIII breaks with Rome and founds Church of England.

1547 Ivan the Terrible comes to power in Russia.

1564–1616 Life of William Shakespeare.

1559 Tobacco first brought to Europe from New World.

1543 Copernicus' book on cosmos published.

1571 Battle of Lepanto – end of Ottoman sea power in Mediterranean.

1568–1648 Dutch revolt from Spain.

1609 Galileo confirms that the sun is at the center of the solar system.

1609 Dutch republic becomes independent.

1620 First weekly newspapers in Europe (Amsterdam).

1609 Telescope invented by Dutchman Hans Lipperman.

1630 Dutch art at its greatest: Rembrandt (1606– 1669), Vermeer (1632– 1675)

1628 William Harvey discovers the circulation of blood.

1510 Beginning of transatlantic slave trade organized by Portuguese.

1546 Mali Empire destroyed by Songhai.

1570–1610 Kanem-Bornu kingdom in central Africa allies with Ottomans.

1578 Moroccans destroy Portuguese bases in North-western Africa.

1600s Hausa Kingdom dominates trade routes across the Sahara.

1590 Moroccans invade Songhai Empire.

1620s Queen Nzinga of Ndongo fights Portuguese in Angola (above).

COME TO THINK OF IT...

became a stream, which ran quickly around the world.

Like everyone else, the Pole Nicolaus Copernicus (*left*) thought the sun, stars, and planets went around the Earth. But when he tried to discover exactly how this happened, he got nowhere. So he tried pretending the Earth went around the sun. He did his math again... and bingo – everything worked out just right. The Earth really did spin around the sun! Nicolaus felt dizzy and sick, and kept his discovery a secret until his death in 1543.

For thousands of years really good ideas – such as wheels or decimals – didn't come along very often. They fell in slow drips, about one every 500 years, plopping mostly onto China or the Middle East, then trickling out to other places. Around 1400, this changed: Europeans took over as the "no.1 ideas people;" the drip of new ideas and inventions

In 1609, Italian Galileo Galilei proved Nicolaus right by looking up at heavenly bodies through his new telescope. Dutchman Anton van Leeuwenhoek preferred to gaze at tiny earthly bodies, through his microscope (1674). Europeans also looked into human bodies – in England, William Harvey found that blood went around and around, like water in a radiator (1628).

Key Men
For most of history, learning was rare and quite secret. The German Johannes Gutenberg invented the modern printing press (about 1440), and a flood of cheap books gave everyone the key to knowledge.

Sir Francis Bacon (1561–1626) unlocked science: Instead of doing experiments to back up an idea, he said we should start with experiments, then come up with theories to fit the facts.

Ship Shapes
In the 10th century, the Vikings crossed the Atlantic Ocean in open longships. Decked 15th-century European vessels were rounder and more comfortable.

The first European to make gunpowder was smoky friar Roger Bacon (died 1292). Within 100 years, soldiers were stuffing it into metal tubes to make guns. This invention allowed the Spanish, French, English, Dutch, and Portuguese not just to visit other lands but to steal them. (Guns vs. spears = no contest.)

Western Europeans stole other people's ideas and expanded them. Adding the triangular sail from the Mediterranean to their own idea of the tiller, they made ships to sail the oceans.

They borrowed the compass from China and the Arab astrolabe to figure out where they were going, then wrote it down on a chart.

In 1569, Gerardus Mercator put maps and charts together to make an atlas. He imagined the round world as a giant orange, then unpeeled it to draw it on flat paper (*above*).

As well as nasty inventions, Europeans came up with lots of useful ideas, such as pencils instead of chalk, and fireplaces, stoves, and chimneys instead of bonfires in the middle of the living room. They also made carts with swiveling axles that could steer around corners (*below*).

Time Machines
Until the 14th century, most people couldn't tell the time because there wasn't a time to tell – there was a time but no one knew what it was. The first clocks had only an hour hand. When people were still late for dinner, minute hands were added (about 1400), then second hands (about 1550).

FLEAS AND FLORINS

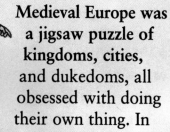

Medieval Europe was a jigsaw puzzle of kingdoms, cities, and dukedoms, all obsessed with doing their own thing. In Russia, various czars (Caesars) of the Mongol-mangled Moscow-dwellers struggled to create a state of their own. In central Europe, the Byzantines and Bulgars fought bloody battles. Despite joining with Poland (1386), by 1494 the gigantic Lithuania had been swallowed by Russia.

Spain squeezed the Muslims back into Africa by 1492. Meanwhile, various king Louis stuck France together. Italian-speakers remained in their cozy little towns. The Germans did the same, but said they were ruled by a Holy Roman Emperor. The Jews had no place to go, so everyone picked on them.

The kings of England tried to force the Welsh and Scots to join them. When the brave-hearted Scots refused, from 1337–1453 assorted Edwards and Henrys used longbows to make the French become English instead (The 100 Years' War). They failed (*above*).

With so many languages, customs, and costumes, Christianity was about the only thing Europeans had in common.

Most used the pope-led (Roman Catholic) type. Russians, Greeks, and a few others preferred the pope-less (Orthodox) variety. This made the Jews feel even more left out.

CHOPPER STOPPER
Europeans chopped down trees to clear land for farming. This meant more food and more people kept alive – until black blobs appeared on people. These marked a deadly plague – the Black Death – that came with fleas that rode on rats that sailed in ships from the East. Thirty million flea-bitten Europeans died (1348–1352).

As the Church issued passports to heaven, everyone tried to keep it happy with gifts of land, money, etc. These made the Catholic Church rich, fat, and lazy. Poping was so popular that there were once three popes at the same time. By 1500, the Church (and the pope) was so rich, fat, and lazy that it almost forgot what it was there for.

Furious protesters flicked through their cheap, printed Bibles. Not finding anything about fat popes, they (Protestants) took all the church wealth they could grab and set up their own Christianities. The pope-ites (Roman Catholics) fought back. Religious wars rumbled on for almost 500 years.

LEO SUPER DOODLE
Leonardo da Vinci (1452–1519) was a painter, sculptor, scientist, engineer, and architect. For fun he filled his doodle pad with extraordinary inventions – such as a flying machine – that were 400 years too early.

When they weren't fighting or plague-dodging, Europeans were getting richer. At first the Italian cities such as Venice and Florence did best. They set up banks with paper money (1600s) and, later, stocks, shares, and insurance.

The Best at Being Bad
The Italian Borgia family (left) beat all-comers in the early modern pentathlon: plotting, feasting, murder, treachery, and general wickedness.

It wasn't long before the moneymaking craze spread north, to places like London, Paris, and Amsterdam. By 1550, most Europeans spent more time counting florins (*right*) than clanking about in armor.

Wealthy Europeans sponsored artists and scholars. Starting in Italy, a wave of wacky paintings, plays, poems, statues, and pretty ceilings swept the continent. It even swept into barbaric Britain, where Shakespeare made playing an art (*left*). This culture craze was misnamed the rebirth (Renaissance) of ancient civilization – thanks to the Arabs, the old ways had never been forgotten.

I AM IMPORTANT
Europeans loved having their portraits painted. This suggested that every individual – prince and pauper, man or woman – was worth bothering about.

The Perfect Gentleman
The ideal Renaissance man was brilliant at everything from tennis and painting to poetry and sword-fighting.

HELLO SAILOR

Once they had farms and homes, most humans weren't eager to leave them. The Pacific canoeists always had itchy feet (or paddles), and occasionally nosy folk such as Italy's Marco Polo (1254–1324) or China's Zheng He (1370–1433) had wandered over the horizon.

Greedy conquerors (e.g., Mongols) also went looking for new victims. But by and large, humans were a stay-at-home type of species. This changed in the 15th century.

The Portuguese went first, creeping around Africa to India and the Far East (by 1509). They dropped off Christianity and tin trinkets and returned with silk and spices. The Spanish, led by Italian Christopher Columbus, crossed the Atlantic and stumbled into America (1492). They gave smallpoz to the locals and grabbed silver in return (*bottom right*), so they decided to stay. The French, Dutch, and English followed soon afterward.

Gold Grabbers
The Europeans who searched the New World for El Dorado ("the golden land") were not the kind of people to bump into on a dark night.

For all kinds of reasons, most not very pleasant, large numbers of Europeans boarded their boats and sailed off to look at the rest of the world. They liked what they found (land and gold) so they took it.

Since they had guns and horses, there wasn't much anyone could do about it – apart from poisoning Europeans with a secret weapon (tobacco) or plaguing them with a nasty disease (syphilis).

By 1650, busy wooden ships freckled the oceans. Most of the world was accurately on the map (except Australia), and groups of greedy Europeans were living in almost every corner of it.

Chris' Tiny Tub
If you put a modern super-tanker (500,000 tons) on one side of a set of scales and 5,000 Santa Marias (Columbus' flagships) on the other, what would you get? A perfect balance!

POLES AND PARTIES

European rulers made a habit of trying to grab each other's goodies. The half-Spanish, half-German Holy Roman Emperor (HRE) Charles V (1519–1558) was the most powerful person of his time.

So he decided that as he wasn't Holy or Roman (his empire was mostly German), at least he could be a proper Emperor. But when he tried to join his lands together, everyone else ganged up against him.

Several other rulers tried to climb the greasy European pole. Philip II of Spain (1556–1598) was also pulled down by smaller countries hanging onto his heels.

When Catholic French kings (such as Francis I) had a turn at the pole, they slipped down on homemade, Protestant grease. Europeans were excellent at making religion an excuse for not loving their neighbors.

The little sailor nations in the top left-hand corner of Europe (England, Holland, and Sweden) didn't want to win the greasy pole game. But they didn't want anyone else to win either. They were perfectly happy to get richer and richer.

TOP EUROPEAN

CHARLES HRE

FRANCIS I

PHILIP II

IVAN

AUSTRIA

F. I

OTTOMANS

DUTCH

The Swedes bagged bits of land around the Baltic Sea. The Dutch threw out their Spanish masters (1648) and concentrated on shipping. The English borrowed Scottish kings, got fed up with them, and tried running things without a king (page 83). Civil war became party war (Whigs vs. Tories) and everyone who was anyone got a say in government.

On the other side of the continent, assorted Ivans – Terrible (1547–1584) and otherwise – were

MEANWHILE...
Queen Elizabeth I of England (1558–1603) made a name for herself ("Virgin Queen") for refusing a marriage partner, while Ottoman Emperor Suleiman the Magnificent (1520–1566) had a whole houseful (his harem).

turning Russia into a possible pole-climber – and a certain Pole-basher. Meanwhile, Austrians and Hungarians were deafened by Turks hammering at the gates of Vienna (1683).

JOGGERS AND SCRUBBERS

Quipu

Of all the gloomy numbers thrown up in the history lottery, the Aztecs were about the gloomiest. They piled into Mexico in the 13th century, roughed up the natives and set up a massive island base – Tenochtitlán – in the middle of Lake Texcoco.

The Aztecs were great traders and builders. What made them so gloomy was their evil sun-god, Horrible Huitzilopochtli. They believed that the only way to stop him from destroying the world was to feed him a special type of honey found in the blood of human hearts.

Heavenly Hoax?
The Aztecs believed in Quetzalcoatl. To them he was a bearded, white-skinned god who one day would appear from the east. When bearded, white-skinned (and most ungodlike) Spaniards appeared in the 16th century, the Aztecs didn't know whether this was a heavenly hoax or the real thing.

The Aztecs used their neighbors as a blood bank, so they loved a good revolt. It gave their jaguar and eagle warriors an excuse to bring in captives to maintain Huitzilopochtli's heart rate. The record offering was 20,000 hearts per day (hpd).
Understandably, the neighbors grew heartily sick of being simply numbers in the "hpd rate."

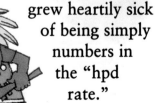

The Incas of Peru were altogether more cheerful than the Aztecs. Led by Super-Inca Pachacuti, in the 15th century they expanded their empire and tidied it up.
They arranged people in neat units (1 unit = 10 families), and made sure that they worked hard and behaved. Slim state joggers carried messages on a 12,000-mile network of litter-free roads. Everything that happened was carefully recorded with knots in pieces of colored string (quipu).

Maya Empire (page 50)

Aztec Empire (Mexico)

When the Europeans reached America and realized that it wasn't China, they called it the New World. Of course, it was the same age as everywhere else in the world, but it was new to them.
They gawked at its turkeys and tomatoes, they marveled at Inca organization and the towering Aztec temples. But what impressed them most of all was its gold and silver.

The Spaniards were first to cash in. Hernan Cortés crushed the Aztecs (1521), Francisco Pizarro pulverized the Incas (1532). Galleon after galleon sailed home to Spain laden with riches. After the soldiers came missionaries and settlers. Soon the European way of life had been transported to America – clothing, dogs, diseases, and all.

Because it was largely empty space, the Spanish and Portuguese didn't think much of North America. The British, French, and Dutch had other ideas. The North not only supplied useful things like furs and turkeys, but was an ideal dumping ground for misfits.

Puritans were considered to be the most awkward misfits. They wanted to scrub Protestantism clean of its last bits of popery, such as bishops. Most people liked their religion muddled. So, the Puritans went to North America (like the Pilgrim Fathers in 1620) to set up squeaky clean, Catholic-free settlements of their own

Slave Trade
Conquerors are an unpleasant group. When the European settlers in America and the Caribbean needed more workers, they bought African slaves at bargain rates and shipped them like cattle across the Atlantic. The trade in slaves brought millions to a few and misery to millions.

Long-distance state joggers

Andes Mountains

Inca Empire

The Slim Empire
Bordered by the Andes, the Incas had the longest, thinnest empire ever.

MONGOL, MING, AND MANCHU

The Chinese were used to thinking that they were the world's no. 1 people, so they were shattered to find Mongol khans from the other side of the wall on their throne. But the khans were not kind and rumblings soon suggested that even heaven wanted a change.

In 1368, military monk Chu Yuan-chang swapped Ming for Mongols. Chu realized that for the Ming to last, they had to be popular. He repaired the Great Wall and built up the army to keep out the Mongols. Slavery was abolished and chubby landlords were slimmed down and their fat given to the peasants.

For about a century, everything Ming went swimmingly. Its armies stretched China's borders. Zheng He's junks sailed to Africa, and returned with tribute and giraffes (1431–1433).

Smiled on by culture vulture Emperor Yong Le (1402–1424), artists potted and painted as never before.

Ming magnificence did not last. Idle emperors closed the door on the rest of the world. The great oceangoing ships rotted into junk heaps. Selfish, thick-skinned mandarins (officials) plotted and schemed. By the 17th century the peasants (and heaven) were grumbling again, while in the north the pig-tailed Manchu sharpened their swords, gazed at the Great Wall, and wondered...

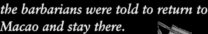

MINGLING WITH THE MING
The Ming looked down their noses at foreigners. The Portuguese were allowed to set up a base at Macao (1557), and for a while Christian missionaries mingled at court.

But once the Chinese had what they wanted (brass cannons and a new calendar), the barbarians were told to return to Macao and stay there.

"CANNON" LAW

The watery side of the world (Southeast Asia and the Pacific) was in turmoil. Japan was in chaos. Its emperors were useless, its shoguns sloppy (page 49), and its ordinary people plagued with pirates, soldiers, and pushy Europeans. The din contrasted strangely with the silky silence of the Japanese court. By 1591, Hideyoshi Toyotomi got things under control again. He then handed

over to the tough Tokugawa shoguns (1603). They threw out the Europeans and settled Japan down for 250 years (the Great Peace).

The rest of Asia remained very much awake. Fed up with being bossed around by foreigners, Korean Yi Song-gye drove out first the Mongols and then the Chinese. Yi-faithful Koreans accepted his Yi dynasty (1392) and created a culture of their own. They replaced the tricky Chinese alphabet and moved their base to Seoul.

MEANWHILE...
While New Zealand Maoris were settling down in fortified pas,

the Ming were hiding from Mongols behind their Great Wall,

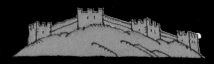

and Europeans were safe from bouncing cannonballs in their slanted-walled forts.

King Trailok (1448–1488) pieced together Siam (now Thailand). He kept his people happy by sharing pieces of his kingdom with them. Meanwhile, by 1560, Kings Tabinshwehti and Bayinnaung created a bumper Burma state that included Mons, Pagans, and some northern Siamese.

Europeans sniffed around the Pacific for spices. Needing places to rest and bag up their nutmeg, they used guns to blast toeholds in Asia (e.g. Malacca, 1511). By 1650, islanders and aborigines across the Pacific were learning cannon law. They didn't like it, but they didn't have much choice.

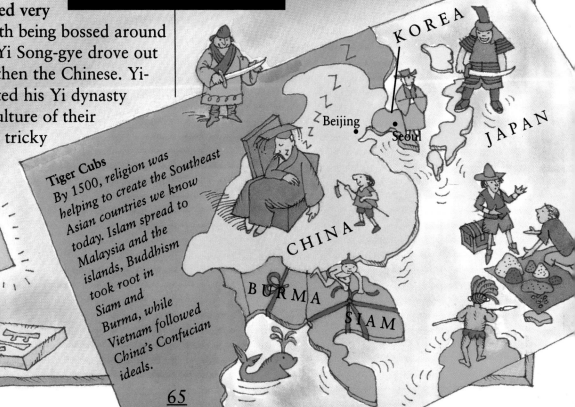

Tiger Cubs
By 1500, religion was helping to create the Southeast Asian countries we know today. Islam spread to Malaysia and the islands, Buddhism took root in Siam and Burma, while Vietnam followed China's Confucian ideals.

FOUNDING AND SIKHING

Timur Lenk

Babar

Fourteenth-century India was breaking up. Invaders streamed in through the holes. First came Timur Lenk, who sacked Delhi and moved swiftly on to avoid the stinking corpses. Then his relative, Babar the Afghan, bounded in to found the Mogul Empire (in 1526).

The Muslim Moguls were generally good news. Babar was an avid gardener, reader, and writer. His grandson Akbar (1549–1605) wasn't bookish, but he was a better soldier and really wise. He married a Hindu, encouraging Hindus and Muslims to stop squabbling, and tried to ban the nasty habit of burning widows (*below*).

Akbar even chatted with visiting Christians. He wasn't impressed with their religion, but he approved of decorating top people with halos – from Emperor Jahangir onward all emperors wore halos. Of the later Moguls, Shah Jahan stands out for splashing out on the most beautiful tomb in the world – the Taj Mahal (completed 1650) – in memory of his favorite wife, Mumtaz Mahal.

Following the emperor's example, Muslims and Hindus got along much better. Some Hindus found their one god Rama, while Guru Nanak sought truth in Sikhism, which was genuinely a one-god faith.

The new mood was spoiled by Aurungzeb the Grumpy (1658–1707), who went back to Hindu-hating. Another worry was that their European visitors looked as if they had no intention of leaving.

Honeyville
The Golden Temple at Amritsar (right) is the holiest Sikh shrine (built 1604). It stands in the middle of a lake from which the town gets its name – "the pool of nectar."

MIGHTY MUSLIMS

The Byzantine Empire lay like a forgotten old coat left in the southeast corner of Europe.

Plague carried off its citizens and Turks carried off its lands. By 1400, only the city of Constantinople was left. Finally, Muhammad II knocked down the walls, charged in, and killed the last emperor (1453). The Roman Empire had truly fallen at last.

The Sunni Muslims who grabbed Byzantium were the Osmanlis (now called Ottomans), the hardiest of the many varieties of Turk. They had started out under border lord Osman I (about 1300) and in fifty years gobbled up all of Turkey (Asia Minor).

After a skirmish with Timur Lenk, they had dusted themselves off and begun again. By 1550, the well-run empire of Suleiman the Super Turk stretched from the Indian Ocean to Vienna.

It was managed by officials who didn't care what people believed, as long as they behaved (*below*).

The Shiite Safanids of Persia were on the make, too. Shah Ismail got them going (1501), despite losing a Sunni vs. Shiite match with the Ottomans and never smiling again. The supreme Safanid was the busy Shah Abbas I

HEALTH WARNING
To bash his way into Byzantium, Muhammad II used the longest, heaviest, noisiest cannon ever. It took 2,000 men to move it. Pregnant women were said to have blocked their ears when it fired, in case the bang made them give birth.

(1588–1629), who sat in his new headquarters at Isfahan and smiled over an empire of culture and carpets. His successors were less active (politically) and drifted off into the harem.

Safanid Empire

Mogul Empire

Ottoman Empire

Constantinople

Isfahan

Mecca

The Big Three
Three Muslim empires dominated central Asia in the 17th century.

MARKET FORCES

From about 1450, the rest of the world started taking Africa much more seriously. And Africans, whether they liked it or not, had to think more seriously about the rest of the world.

For a long time, Islam had tied North and West Africa to Asia. The gold-rich empires of Mali and Songhai were at the front of the Afro-Muslim store window. Sonni Ali (1462–1492) brought the Songhais out of Mali's shadow. Muhammad Turré then built them up with taxes, waterworks, and a police force before Moroccans spoiled his handiwork at the end of the 16th century. ▶

Since Sumer time (page 20), Africa had happily shared her many goodies with outsiders. By the 15th century, herds of camels were trekking north across the Sahara with loads of gold, salt, tusks, and ebony, then plodding back again with carefully-wrapped Chinese pottery and silks. In the east, Arab ships sailed back and forth with similar cargoes.

By the middle of the 16th century, Europeans were haggling away beside the Arabs in most of the markets of Africa. At the top of the Portuguese shopping list was not gold but slaves for export to Brazil. ▶

Desert Bouncers
The Mali and Songhai Empires used heavy cavalry to control trade routes across the Sahara.

DESIGNER SONGHAI
Of all the pilgrims who trekked to Mecca, none turned more heads than the trendy ruler of the Songhai Empire. When he opened his skin luggage designer leopard handfuls of gold dished out the sensation coins, he became the of the season.

Hop It!
A Moroccan army invaded the Songhai Empire in 1590. To show that they were not afraid of Moroccan guns, the Songhai soldiers tied up one leg.

Business Queen Nzinga of Ndongo (Angola) began trading with the Europeans in 1623. She pointed out that if she let traders go on buying people, the shelves would soon be empty, and her Ndongans were not for sale. The Portuguese ignored her and grabbed what they could get. Nzinga closed up shop and spent the next 40 years fighting them.

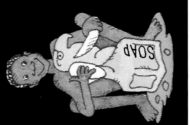

MEANWHILE...
While Zimbabweans were chipping out birds from soapstone, Pacific islanders were carving mystical figures in wood, Chinese were molding clay animals onto their roof tiles, and Italians were sculpting naked men out of marble.

Compared with the blood and bullying of the rest of the continent (and almost everywhere else in the world), southern Africa was probably quite a happy place to live. The remote Lubalanders, safe from merchants and missionaries, puttered around on their farms. Not far away, the Zimbabweans ("stone house people"), built a town of towers and cozy thatched huts (1100–1500), protected by thick walls that didn't always match up.

Sharp traders
Many Central African tribes carried huge spear heads and throwing knives. These were not weapons but items for trade!

The Ottomans sat comfortably on North Africa and used its ports to jump on passing Christian ships. Muslims even managed to clamber up into hilly Ethiopia for the first time (1529). A few years later, the Ethiopians hired muscular Portuguese to push them back down again.

Gun-waving Portuguese were throwing their weight around elsewhere. They grabbed Sofala in East Africa and snipped off pieces of the West Coast. Startled, some Africans (e.g. the king of Kongo) made friends with the new arrivals and accepted their Christian god.

Bang On
Ancient African drum patterns led to the rock and pop rhythms of the 20th century.

Other states, like Kanem-Bornu in central Africa, believed Allah had more to offer and signed up with the Ottoman camel corps (1570–1610).

5 AND THEN...

THE SHAPE OF THINGS TO COME

The exciting new "sport" of revolution was invented during this period (1650–1800). It soon became immensely popular all over the world and is still played to this day.

The reason why revolution caught on was that everyone could play, each game was different, and it could be played in all kinds of situations. The only thing that all games of revolution had in common was that when they finished, nothing was ever the same again.

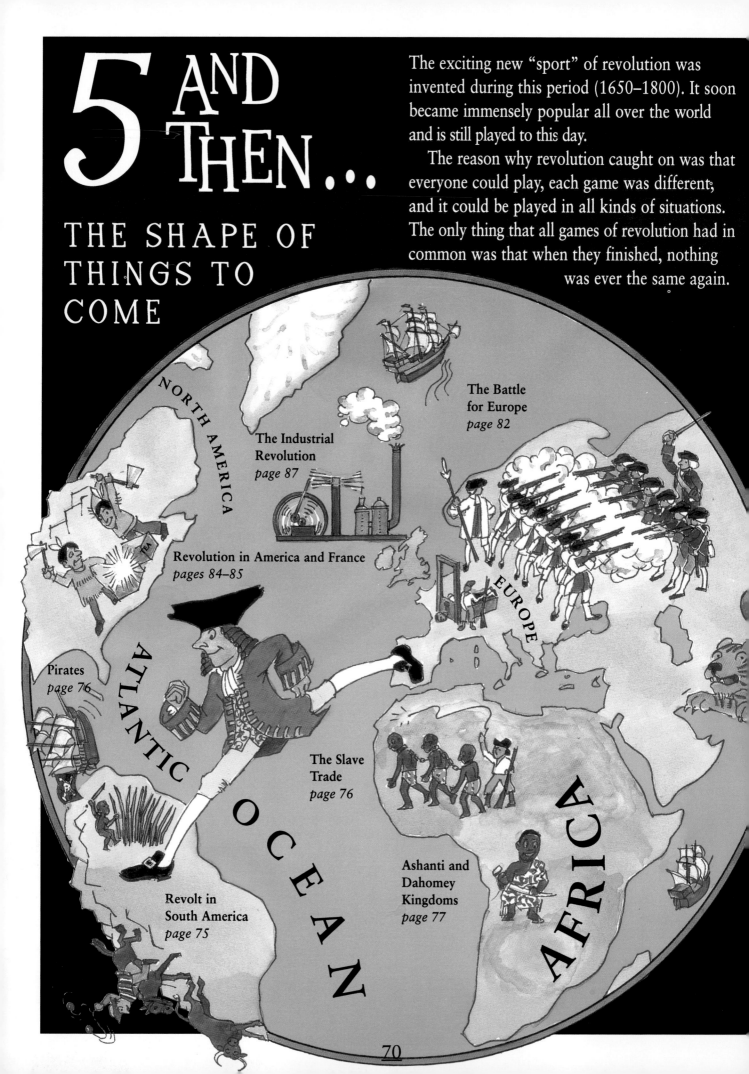

NORTH AMERICA

The Battle
for Europe
page 82

The Industrial
Revolution
page 87

Revolution in America and France
pages 84–85

EUROPE

Pirates
page 76

ATLANTIC

The Slave
Trade
page 76

OCEAN

AFRICA

Ashanti and
Dahomey
Kingdoms
page 77

Revolt in
South America
page 75

Americans and French played political revolution. They used kings, queens, guns, and guillotines. It was very exciting – particularly for the winners – but also dangerous. Quieter countries, like England and Holland, chose to play agricultural revolution. This was slower than the political version, but had the big advantage that almost everyone won.

Finally, there was industrial revolution, which the British invented. The game was messy, but winners made a lot of money. Only when the game had been played for 200 years did scientists realize it needed a health warning. Even people not playing revolution, such as the Chinese, Russians, and South Americans, were getting their boards and pieces ready for games later on.

Russian Conquests
page 82

NORTH AMERICA

Buffalo Hunters
page 74

Qing Dynasty China
page 80

The Last of the Mogul Emperors
page 78

PACIFIC OCEAN

Burma and Thailand
page 81

Australia and Convicts
page 81

INDIAN OCEAN

1625 A.D. TO 1800 A.D.

| 1625 | 1650 | 1675 | 1700 |

AMERICA

1655 Britain captures Jamaica (soon home to pirates, left) from the Spanish.

1664 New Amsterdam is taken by the British from the Dutch. They later rename it New York.

1654 The Dutch are driven out of Brazil by Portugal.

1679 French priest Louis Hennepin reaches the Niagara Falls in Canada.

1681–1682 Frenchman Robert La Salle explores the Mississippi River from source to mouth and founds Louisiana.

1693 Gold found in Brazil.

1700s Caribbean sugar plantations bring sugar to the world (left).

1700s With Native American help, European settlers begin to prosper in North America.

1711 Settlers and Native Americans fight a war in North Carolina.

ASIA

1645 Taj Mahal built in Agra, India.

1644 Manchus found Qing Dynasty in China.

1661–1722 Qing (Manchu) Emperor Kangxi encourages arts in China.

1658–1707 Reign of Aurungzebe – last great Mogul ruler in India. After his death, empire begins to break up.

1674 Sivaji builds Hindu Maratha Kingdom in southern India.

1690 British East India Company founds city of Calcutta in northeast India.

1700s First contact between Tahitians and Europeans.

1716–1745 Reforming shogun Tokugawa Yoshimune rules Japan.

1724 Hyderaba (Deccan) leaves Mogul Empire.

AFRICA

1650s Portuguese fight Muslim Africans near Zambezi River.

1662 Destruction of Kongo Kingdom by Portuguese.

1660s Mawlay-al-Rashid restores Sultanate in Morocco.

1652 Foundation of Cape Colony by Dutch settlers.

1670s French settle in Senegal.

1680s and 1690s Rise of West African kingdoms of Ashanti (Ghana) and Dahomey (Benin).

1698 Portuguese forced out of Mombasa on African east coast.

1701 Osei Tutu creates free Ashanti nation in West Africa, with a capital at Kumasi.

1705 Hussain ibn Ali founds state of Tunis in North Africa.

EUROPE

1643–1715 Reign of Louis XIV of France (Sun King, below).

1660 Classical period of French culture: Molière (playright, 1622–73); Poussin (painter 1594–1665); Couperin (composer, 1668–1733).

1648 Peace of Westphalia ends Thirty Years' War in Europe.

1642–49 English Civil War ends in execution of King Charles I.

1682–1725 Reign of Peter the Great of Russia.

1683 Ottoman siege of Vienna is beaten off by Poles.

1689 William of Orange becomes British king.

1687 Isaac Newton publishes his great scientific work Principia.

1701–1713 War of the Spanish Succession; the French are defeated by Britain's Duke of Marlborough at the Battles of Blenheim (1704) and Ramillies (1706).

1712 Thomas Newcomer invents steam pump for use in mines.

1700s Agricultural Revolution (left) spreads in Britain – later to Europe.

1700 Great age of German baroque music: Bach (1685–1750) and Handel (1685–1759).

1725   **1750**   **1775**   **1800**

1736 *Natural rubber is found in the Peruvian rainforests.*

1760 *French possessions in Canada go to Britain (below).*

1776 *American Declaration of Independence.*

1782 *Tupac Amaru leads revolt against Spanish in Peru.*

1742 *Atahualpa II leads Native Americans in Peru in an unsuccessful revolt against the Spanish.*

1781 *British surrender at Yorktown ends American Revolution.*

1773 *Boston Tea Party.*

1789 *George Washington becomes first President of the United States (left).*

1727 *Diamonds discovered in Brazil.*

1727 *Europeans plant first coffee in Brazil.*

1754–1763 *War between Britain and France in North America.*

1775 *American Revolution begins.*

1790s *Revolt in Haiti against French rule, led by Toussaint L'Ouverture.*

1736–1796 *Under Emperor Qianlong the Chinese Empire reaches its greatest extent.*

1750 *Chinese rule begins in Tibet.*

1768–1777 *General Phya Taksin unites Siam.*

1788 *British colony of Australia founded.*

1739 *Nader Kuli attacks India and sacks Delhi, taking Peacock Throne of Mogul emperors.*

1767 *Burma invades Siam.*

1799 *Ranjit Singh creates Sikh Kingdom in Punjab.*

1768–1779 *English captain James Cook explores the Pacific.*

1782–1809 *Rama I king in Thailand.*

1736–1747 *Reign of Nader Kuli as shah of Safanid (Persian) Empire.*

1763 *Treaty of Paris makes Britain major European power in India.*

1818 *British defeat Marathas and become rulers of India.*

1796 *British conquer island of Ceylon.*

1725 *Largest encyclopedia (right) ever written, written for Qing Emperor Yongzheng.*

1757 *British defeat Siuraj-ud-Dawlah, Nawab of Bengal, at Battle of Plassey in India.*

1722–1723 *Ashanti overrun Bono-Mansu regions in west Africa.*

1750–1800 *Europeans begin exploration of Africa: in west 1795–1796 Scotsman Mungo Park travels through Gambia and reaches mouth of Niger River; in east 1768–1773 Scotsman James Bruce explores Ethiopia.*

1800 *Half the people of Brazil now come from Africa.*

1724–1734 *King Agaja of Dahomey stops the slave trade. But it starts again in 1740s.*

1740s *Rise of Lunda Kingdom in central Africa (Zaire /Zambia).*

By 1800 More than 10 million Africans are shipped to America by slavers.

1768 *Ali Bey makes himself sultan of Egypt.*

1798 *Napoleon attacks Egypt.*

1721–1742 *Robert Walpole becomes Britain's first Prime Minister.*

1756–1763 *Seven Years' War: Prussia and Britain fight France, Austria, and Russia.*

1789 *French Revolution begins.*

1792 *French Republic created – start of Revolutionary Wars.*

1740–1786 *Frederick the Great makes Prussia a major power in Europe.*

c.1770 *Advance in technology: Priestly (chemist, 1733–1804); Lavoisier (chemist, 1743–1794); Volta (physicist and chemist, 1745–1827); Harrison invents very accurate timepiece (1762); Watt invents steam engine (1769); Arkwright invents water-powered spinning machine (1769).*

1795 *Poland divided between Russia, Austria, and Prussia.*

1762–1796 *Catherine the Great (left) rules Russia.*

1793 *Decimal system introduced.*

1796 *Jenner discovers smallpox vaccine (left).*

1760s *European Enlightenment: Voltaire (French philosopher, 1694–1778); Rousseau (French philosopher, (1712–88); Hume (English philosopher, 1711–1766).*

c.1790 *Great era of European music: Mozart (1756–1791); Hadyn (1732–1827); and Beethoven (1770–1827).*

1750–1795 *Robert Bakewell uses selective breeding to grow bigger pigs.*

BUZZING

With the arrival of swarms of Europeans and Africans, America buzzed with activity. By about 1800, only in the remotest regions were Native Americans left alone: the Inuits enjoyed an icy isolation in the refrigerated North, while a barrier of snakes, swamp, and illness protected the peoples of the South American jungles.

Inuits

Plains Tribes

First American Colonies

South America

By 1650, the Europeans were shoving Native Americans off their land and their god down their throats. When the Americans objected, European gunslingers beat Native axeswingers every time.

NONSENSE NAME
When Columbus landed in what is now the West Indies, he did not realize he had come to America. He thought he was in the East Indies, so he called the people he met "Indians."

In the early 17th century, European visitors and the North Americans got along quite well. The residents taught the visitors useful tricks, such as corn growing and how to walk on snow. In return, the residents learned what a horse was and how to ride it.

This was such fun that they swapped farming for buffalo hunting and galloped around the prairies to see who their other neighbors were. The fun ended when the visitors began to call themselves residents.

British and French settlers also squabbled among themselves (*above*). The British bagged 13 coastal colonies. The French, helped by their Native American pals, slipped around behind and began waving their flag over Canada and the Mississippi River. By 1750, they were ready to heave the British into the sea.

But the advancing French and company fell foul of British Prime Minister Pitt. He paid his European friends Prussia and Austria to keep the French busy at home in a Seven Years' War (1756–1763), while British General Wolfe ate up Canada and everywhere east of the Mississippi.

Signing Up
As many different languages were spoken on the Plains, American tribes developed a special sign language to keep in touch (left).

The Caribbean is one of the Earth's most pleasant spots. It is not surprising, therefore, that the happy-go-lucky residents (Caribs and Arawaks) were forced to share their island paradises with others.

By about 1800, ravaged by pistols and pox, the unfortunate Caribs and Arawaks existed in name only. The new Caribbeans (*top*) were a colorful mixture of sugar planters, pirates, and slaves (escaped and otherwise).

Since the British filled their colonies with people they didn't really care for, they didn't pay much attention to what they were up to.

The Spanish and Portuguese didn't care much for their colonists, either. But they did mind what they mined. The groans of the slaves digging silver, gold, and diamonds in the New World kept the merchants of the Old World grinning all the way to the bank.

The Spanish court sent out a string of hoity-toity sub-kings (viceroys) to keep colonials and their slaves humble, grateful, hard-working, etc.

By 1782, the ex-Spaniards and ex-Incas, led by Tupac Amaru, were so fed up with all this long-range snooping that they rebelled (*below*). The revolt failed. Nevertheless, it forced the Spanish to watch their step in the future.

BITTERSWEET
Medieval Europe was a bitter place – a lick of honey was the sweetest treat most people ever tasted. So when cheap sugar came pouring over from New World sugar cane plantations (from 1650 onward), they went sugar crazy. They boiled it into candy, piled it in puddings, stirred it into tea, coffee, and chocolate – and brought smiles to the lips of tooth-pullers.

TRADERS AND SLAVERS

European busybodies remained largely outside the African picture. Traders in slaves, gold, and ivory hung around the shores but did not go inland because it was too dark and dangerous for them, and African merchants brought out what they wanted.

Only in the late 18th century did a few inquisitive Britons peer up the river to see if the continent was quite as murky as it appeared from the outside.

The exception was South Africa, settled by Bible-bashing Boers (Dutch farmers) in 1652. By the time the British took over the place a century later, the Boers had persuaded many  Africans that the Christian god was a flying white Dutchman. When the British said this wasn't true, the Boers grew angry and trekked off (1836) to bash Bibles (and Africans) further north.

Sticky Business
One of the major exports from Africa during the 17th century was gum arabic (below). As well as being an excellent glue, it was used in perfumes, candy, and medicine.

MEANWHILE...
While buccaneers were looting Spanish treasure ships in the Caribbean, corsairs from the Algerian coast of North Africa were rounding up European slaves in the Mediterranean, and Ching Chih-Ling terrorized the south coast of China with a fleet of 1,000 junks.

By 1700, the vast Ottoman Empire was fraying like a carpet. The African fringe was held together by governors (*pashas*). Their job was to see that the empire didn't become unraveled from the sultan (*below*).

Local army commanders (beys) had other ideas: The boisterous bey of Algiers made himself into a pasha; Egypt's Ali Bey went one step further and became a sultan (1768). Meanwhile... the Moroccans – never too happy about being told what to do – tried 30 years of no government at all.

To the irritation of Muslims and the amazement of everyone else, Ethiopia (or Abyssinia) remained cut off and Christian just as it had for centuries.

From 1768–1773, Scotsman James Bruce climbed up to Ethiopia to see what was going on. When he got home and wrote down what he had seen, no one believed him.

Soul Survivor (left)
Built in the 13th century, St. George's Church in Lalibela, Ethiopia, was dug 40 feet into the ground.

Some of the most successful **traders and slavers** were the Ashanti (Ghana) and Dahomey (Benin) in the west and Lunda (Zaire/Zambia) in the center. By the 1740s, the Lunda controlled a trading empire exporting slaves to the west and copper and ivory to the east.

Led by vigorous kings (Ashantihene), the Ashanti were particularly powerful. Instead of a flag, they rallied around the Golden Chair of Kumasi, the headquarters. They decorated the Chair with the heads (also golden) of the commanders they had defeated. This showed visitors how tough they were.

TUTU THE NATION-MAKER

Africans preferred fuzzy-edged nations to sharp-edged countries. Nations were more easily set up and saved the hassle of passports. Osei Tutu (1695–1712), chief of the West African Ashanti, was a great nation-maker. After he had nationalized the Ashanti, they kept up his good work with jugs of national spirit at a huge annual party.

Several African nations made a fortune by trading with the rest of the world. But trade also kept Africans at each other's throats. While gold and copper could be dug from the ground and ivory hacked off dead animals, slaves weren't so easy to come by.

Some tribes grew rich by rounding up unsuspecting neighbors and selling them to slavers.

Breaking up the Family
Whole families (right) *were captured and sold to the European traders. Before the journey to the New World, families and tribes were separated to make revolt more difficult.*

RIDING AROUND

Nader then rampaged east through Kabul and Lahore, kicking over the crumbling Mogul Empire as he went. In Delhi he helped himself to the Mogul millions (including the Koh-i-noor diamond) and plunked himself on their Peacock Throne (*below*).

The Ottoman Turks, like all conquerors, rode on the carousel of history. Having risen to great heights, by the 18th century they were slowly swinging down again. The sinking feeling was strongest in the Balkans and around the Black Sea, where hungry Christian states bit large chunks off their empire (*left*). Sleepy sultans also agreed to let Austria and Russia keep an eye on Christians in the Ottoman Empire, to make sure they weren't picked on.

The Persians enjoyed a bit of Turkey, too. The Safanid *shahs* (kings) now spent most of their waking hours in the harem and ignored the antics of vigorous Afghan invaders. Nevertheless, their empire found a new hero in General Nader Kuli. He took Tifilis from the Turks (1735) and went on to make himself shah.

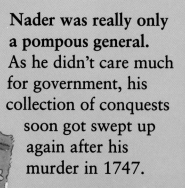

AHMAD THE AFGHAN
Chief Ahmad of the Durrani (1747–1773) built Afghanistan out of the pieces left over by the rampages of Nader Kuli. From his base at Qandahar, Ahmad plundered the Punjab (north India) and mangled the Marathas at Panipat (1761). But one-man empires don't last, and after Ahmad's death Afghanistan shrank back into the mountains.

Nader was really only a pompous general. As he didn't care much for government, his collection of conquests soon got swept up again after his murder in 1747.

The Muslim Mogul Empire in India fell apart like the Ottoman Empire. The East Indian province of Bengal broke away in the early 18th century, and in 1724 southern Hyderabad went its own way under Nizam (prince) Asaf Jah.

The Moguls reached their low point when they lost their precious Peacock Throne.

Europeans had been picking at the borders of India for some time. The British and French were the greediest, so they usually found themselves on opposite sides in Indian battles. In 1756, it looked as if the French had come out on top when their friend Siuraj-ud-Dawlah, the Nawab (ruler) of Bengal, pushed the British out of Calcutta.

COMPANY RULE OK?
In 1601, the British founded the East India Company to trade. It set up bases on the coast, and to guard these, it took over the land next to them. To protect this land, it took more until it governed all of India. To show how much he liked the company, Nawab Tipu Sultan had a model made showing a tiger eating its employees.

But Britain was on the side of the carousel of history going up. Robert Clive, a clever British soldier, squashed Siuraj-ud-Dawlah at the Battle of Plassey (1757). Fifty years later, the British East India Company had most of eastern India on its plate and was busy carving up the rest.

Meanwhile, in west India, Hindu Sivaji had united the Maratha peoples into a state. He had trouble getting Mogul Aurungzeb the Grumpy (*page 66*) to accept this, but escaped by hiding in a basket (*left*). Until they met the British, the Marathas made a good living out of farming, trade, and piracy.

The First Juggernaut
In a tradition that survives today, once a year the 40-ft-high statue of the Hindu god Jagannath was carried through the streets of Puri in northern India on a huge wagon.

EASTERN PROMISE

When the Ming lost Beijing to rebels in 1643, they invited the semi-Chinese Manchu from over the Great Wall to help them get it back. This was the final fling of the Ming: The Manchu threw the rebels out of Beijing and kicked their hosts off the throne. Shunzhi (1644–1661), the first Manchu emperor, named himself after the ancient Qin Dynasty (page 22) to make himself sound Chinese.

The foreign Manchu (Qing) bosses served the Chinese well. By 1792, their armies had bagged useful border areas such as Formosa (Taiwan), Outer Mongolia, Turkestan, and Nepal. The Tibetan Buddhists (*left*) were forced to dance to a Manchu tune (1720) and were taken over completely when they got it wrong.

High Kickers
Painting flourished under the early Qing Dynasty. Also, Beijing Opera, popular after 1800, mixed songs, dance, and even martial arts!

Once they had stamped out old-fashioned Ming thinking, the first few Qing steered China along prosperous new paths. Foreign crops and a new quick-grown rice (*left*) kept more people alive. The doubled population paid the emperors more taxes which they used to help painters, potters, and writers (*right*).

Under Emperor Qianlong (1736–1796), the last great Manchu, China hummed with making and trading. European bargain hunters (still considered barbarians) crowded the bazaar at Guangzhou in the south. But Qianlong lived too long, and by the end of the 18th century Manchu magic was fading fast.

The Crazy Pavilion (above)
Like all rich 19th-century Europeans, the British Prince Regent was crazy about the Orient. His palace at Brighton, England, was a weird jumble of Chinese and Indian styles!

DOUBLE WHAMMY
As far as emperors go, the mighty Manchu Kang-Hsi (1661–1722) and Yongzheng (1722–1735) were as good as one could hope for. They weeded out Ming-minded rebels and corruption, mapped China with missionary help, and planted a blooming culture of arts, crafts, and gigantic encyclopedias.

The Japanese, having peered out at the rest of the world, decided they didn't think much of it. They remained indoors until the middle of the 19th century.

Free from distractions, they concentrated on things they were good at. These included peaceful pastimes (e.g. growing mini-trees, puppet-making, painting, and drama, *top*) and more bloodthirsty ones, like committing *hara-kiri* (ceremonial suicide) and learning to be ninja warriors (*left*).

The bumper Burma bumbled along until the 1760s, when it became tangled up in Siam (Thailand). Phya Taksin persuaded the Siamese they didn't have to be part of the Burmese Empire. But the effort drove him mad, leaving King Rama I to continue the struggle. By the end of his life (1809), Rama (*right*) had finally convinced the Burmese to leave the Siamese for good.

Bow... Wow!
The first Europeans to land in Australia (in 1616) thought kangaroos were jumping dogs!

TICKLISH TATTOOS
Apart from putting up pas and mowing down moas, the one thing the New Zealand Maoris were really good at was carving. They took their chisels to any suitable surface, not only wooden poles and boards but human faces and bottoms!

Far away from these mainland arguments, European sailors were finishing off their map of the Pacific. Steering by clocks and compasses, they found such exotic places as the Sandwich Islands in Hawaii and Tahiti and rushed home with the news. The Polynesians, who'd been there for centuries, wondered what all the fuss was about.

In 1770, James Cook added Australia to the British menu. From 1788–1793 the British used the place as a prison. But when they saw how healthy and empty it was, they encouraged sheep and fresh air enthusiasts to go and keep the convicts company.

SPARKS

By 1650, most of Europe was divided into countries, and its top kings and queens were more enthusiastic than ever about the greasy pole war game. Some smaller states (e.g. Switzerland) preferred to save money (and lives) by watching. Others found they had a better chance of winning in teams (alliances).

The Dutch retired to trading, and painting. According to Spanish writer Miguel de Cervantes (1547–1616), the Spaniards (*right*) wasted their time charging at windmills rather than real enemies. In 1709, Russia pushed Sweden's King Charles down the greasy pole, and by 1795 it had helped to wipe Poland off the map.

When France's Sun King Louis XIV (1643–1715) seemed to have reached the top of the pole, an international army led by Britain's Duke of Marlborough pushed him down again. Louis' wars, palaces, etc. were so costly that he was left ruling a kingdom of penniless skeletons.

Louis XIV
The Sun King

WHO'S RIGHT?
Ordinary people's lives were short and unpleasant. They moaned – and sometimes rebelled – but generally they gritted their teeth and hoped things would turn out better in heaven. Bright philosophers now believed this was wrong. They said everyone (all white males, anyway) had a right to a decent life. Of course, those who were successful disagreed...

In the 18th century, Prussia (a German state) and Russia became key nations. The Prussians made up for their lack of size by organization; the Russians overcame lack of organization by size.

Both countries had to put up with a pair of fiery Great monarchs: Prussia's ruler, the Great Elector, blazed a trail for Frederick the Great (1740–1786); Russia's giant Peter the Great set up a state for Catherine the Great (1762–1796).

Peter Scissorhands
Russia's Czar Peter the Great (almost 7 ft tall) was determined to make Russians look like Europeans. If courtiers refused to shave, he did the snipping himself (above)!

All for One?
Alexandre Dumas' romantic novel The Three Musketeers (1844) ignored the misery and poverty of most 17th-century French people (left).

The British played Hunt the Ruler. After cunning moves by James I and II, Charles I and II, and Oliver Cromwell, Parliament won and crowned a whig-loving Dutchman, William of Orange (in 1689). This left Britain's rulers free to go looking for an empire.

As Europeans were obsessed with the greasy pole game (often played with British money), they didn't notice Britain cruising around the world picking up rich parts of America, India, etc.

French philosophers took note. They said the British way of government was best and tried to switch others to their point of view (the Enlightenment!).

All over the continent, rich men and women drank coffee and discussed how to make government better, kinder, and fairer. Writers filled encyclopedias with enlightened ideas for lighter punishments, brighter prisons, and cleaner peasants. Eager not to be left out, even Frederick and Catherine the Great made enlightened (tolerant) noises, but did little.

Kate the Crusher
Catherine the Great was all in favor of culture and comfort – but not for revolting peasants.

Charlie Gets the Chop
The execution of Britain's Charles I in 1649 dealt a sharp blow to the idea that kings were mini-Gods, but for some time other rulers kept thinking they were heaven-sent.

RHYTHM AND REASON
The brightest bulbs of the Age of Enlightenment were composer Wolfgang Amadeus Mozart (1756–1791) and philosopher François Voltaire (1694–1778). Mozart's music gave reason for delight, Voltaire's writings delighted in reason.

Government changed from a royal hobby to a job for clerks, collectors, officers, and inspectors. Despite the fighting, Europe was getting wealthier and fuller. Cities sprawled, towns crawled, harbors heaved with shipping. A rich gravy of prosperity flowed into the bowls of land owners, boat owners, mine owners, title owners.

Seeing the rich get richer, the poor began to mumble. Lit by sparks of enlightenment, their mumbling grew to a grumbling, then a mighty, rebellious rumbling: "IT'S NOT FAIR!"

RIGHTS, WRONGS, AND REVOLUTIONS

In the 1760s, American colonists were unhappy. Although their British king (George III) lived 3,000 miles away and knew almost nothing about America, he claimed the right to collect their taxes and tell them what to do. Americans said this was the wrong type of right. George stamped about and told them to obey him because he was king.

This made the colonists really annoyed. They held a huge, tea party at Boston (*bottom*), then wrote a Declaration of Independence.

This said that George (*left*) was crazy and that everyone (meaning all white males) was born equal and had a right to be free and happy. To make themselves freer and happier, the 13 colonies had already declared war on England .

George III's soldiers marched about in wigs and tight red uniforms, feeling seasick, homesick, and hot. They were very dashing and wrote songs about how free and wonderful they were.

With help from France and other anti-British countries, they gradually herded the British army into Yorktown. Unable to get away, General Cornwallis' men grew hungrier and hungrier until they finally surrendered. Shortly afterward, the Americans won the war (1781).

This was the American Revolution. The new country – the United States of America – became one of the first republics, or king-free zones. News of what the Americans had done spread rapidly to other countries.

Easy Shooting
British soldiers in the Revolutionary War were nicknamed "Redcoats" because of their bright red uniforms. Unfortunately, this also made them an easy target!

The French listened with great interest. Anything the Americans could do, they decided, they could do better.

Tea Time
In 1773, American colonists dressed up as Mohawk Indians and threw a cargo of tea overboard to show their anger at British taxes.

A Strong Constitution
*In 1787, leading Americans s
down to work out a strong
system of government and t
guarantee citizens' rights.*

Clouds of revolution had been hanging over France for some time. Most French believed it was unfair that a handful of wealthy snobs should have all the fun. In 1789, following the American example, they began to work things out for themselves.

The French Revolution was the biggest and bloodiest yet. Mobs rushed into the streets, robbing the rich, and yelling for liberty, friendship, and equality. They stormed the Bastille prison, a symbol of royal power (*below*), then set up an Assembly (a kind of parliament) to

take away wrongs and dish out rights. In 1792, weak King Louis XVI and his cake-scoffing wife Marie Antoinette were knocked off the throne.

The French Revolution was a runaway train – very exciting but very dangerous. In 1793, it came off the rails when naïve leaders (such as

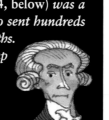

Robespierre) tried to force people to be free. This was the Terror, when the king, queen, and anyone who even thought royal was executed by guillotine.

Foreign armies invaded and France ran out of money and food. Unable to eat rights, the people began wondering whether the Revolution was such a good idea after all.

HONEST GEORGE AND MAD MAX

George Washington led the American Revolution. For a time Maximilien Robespierre led the French Revolution. That's about all they had in common.

Washington (1732–1799, above) was a capital fellow, famous for his honesty. He became the first U.S. President. Robespierre (1758–1794, below) was a fanatic who sent hundreds to their deaths. He ended up having his head cut off by a guillotine.

Experienced leaders brought France back on track in 1794 by doing away with the Revolution's cruel and silly ideas and keeping the rest. They then chose an emperor, Napoléon I (1804–1815), to act like a king, without actually being one.

France's fair laws, rights, etc. were exported all over the world. From now on, although ordinary people's lives might still be short, they did not have to be unpleasant as well.

Chop Chop
The guillotine (left) was the symbol of the French Revolution. Its sharp blade allowed the quick execution of thousands of prisoners accused by radical leaders during the Reign of Terror. Large crowds went to executions to enjoy the gory spectacle.

STEAMING THROUGH THE DAFFODILS

The thing that Homo sapiens sapiens did best was reproduce the species. By 1650 the cast of the human play was 600 million, almost all of them extras. Over the next 150 years, despite efforts to keep numbers down by war, massacre, etc., this had almost doubled to a billion. It was all to do with food.

European (and a few American) farmers led the way. They drained bogs, used machines to sow seed in efficient rows, and freshened fields by swapping crops around and spreading manure (*below*).

Turnips (and potatoes) kept cattle (and people) alive in the winter – a potato plot fed four times as many people as a wheat field. The crossing of meaty male animals with meaty females bred ultra-meaty offspring. This was the Agricultural Revolution.

CREAMY COMPLEXION
Dr. Edward Jenner (b. 1749) wondered why milkmaids didn't get pocked faces like everyone else. The answer, he realized, lay with the cows: People who caught mild cowpox didn't get the killer smallpox. Soon everyone was lining up for a dose of Jenner's cowpox (vaccination).

Brains were buzzing in the laboratory as well as on the farm. Isaac Newton (1642–1727) figured out why rainbows had all the colors in them and why apples fell on his head. Carolus Linnaeus (1707–1778) lined up all the plants and animals he could think of and gave them long Latin names.

French chemist Antoine Lavoisier (1743–1794) founded modern chemistry by discovering oxygen – then had his own supply cut off by the guillotine! Watching dead frogs' legs twitch, Italian Luigi Galvani plugged into the study of electricity in 1786.

Hot Potatoes
The potato was the 18th-century wonder crop. It not only fed lots of people, but tasted great whether baked, boiled, mashed, or fried!

By 1800, European science had spread from the laboratory to the workplace (the Indusrial Revolution).

In England, Abraham Darby used coke (coal residue) in 1709 to heat iron which hardened into metal tough enough for bridges. Watching kettles and slow-thumping steam-pumps, Scotsman James Watt dreamed up the steam engine in 1765. It demanded deep-dug coal for its boilers and measured its muscle in horsepower.

Smash Hit
Inventors came up with some pretty zany ideas. The first person to try roller skates didn't know how to stop and crashed into a mirror!

Humanpower was overtaken, too.
Machines twisted cotton and wool thread finer and quicker than a hundred fingers. Spinning moved from the fireside to riverside factories, where rows of men, women, and children worked long hours amid flapping belts and whirling spindles.

A LOAD OF HOT AIR
Jo and Jack Montgolfier wondered why smoke went up the chimney. When they saw it had to do with hot air (1783), they built a balloon, lit a fire beneath it and sent two passengers soaring off into the blue. The Big Heads had learned to fly!

The old mud roads were now clogged, so engineers built paved, pay-as-you-go roads (turnpikes). Heavy loads of coal and ore slid along freshly-dug canals. The industrious species was becoming an industrial species.

By the late 18th century, after centuries of jogging, change had suddenly broken into a sprint. Romantic poets feared the clamor of the Industrial Revolution was drowning the voice of Nature.

The world, said poet William Wordsworth (1770–1850), was too much with us. He urged people to gaze romantically at Nature and to walk among the daffodils again...

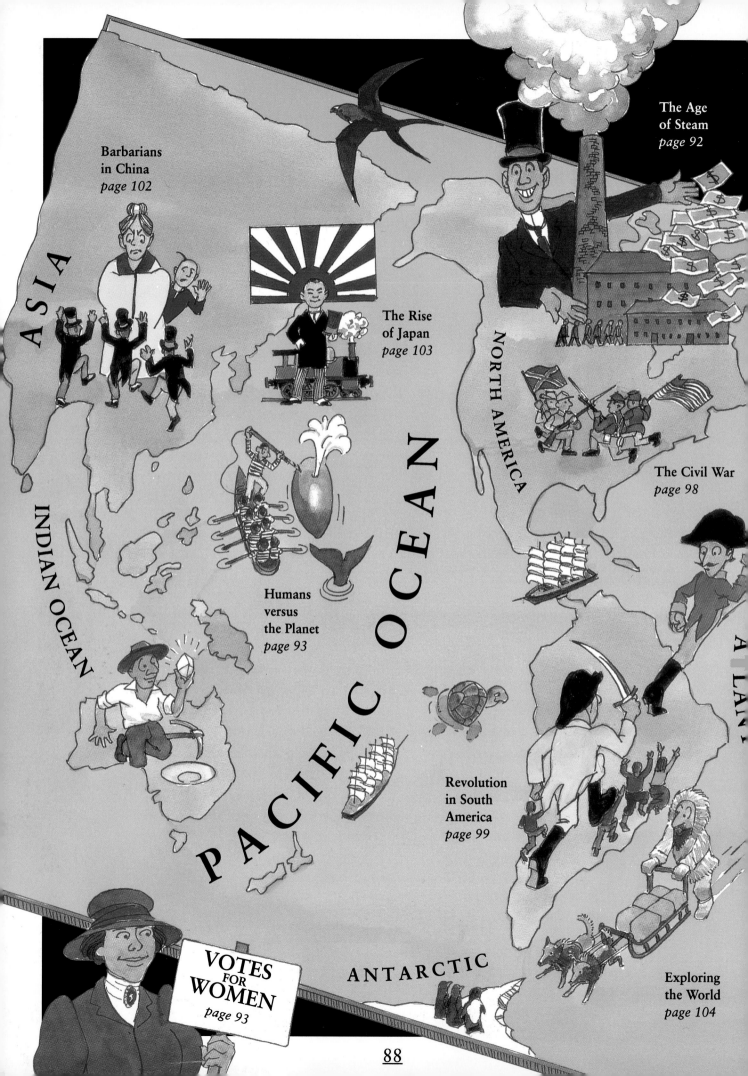

Barbarians
in China
page 102

The Age
of Steam
page 92

ASIA

The Rise
of Japan
page 103

NORTH AMERICA

The Civil War
page 98

INDIAN OCEAN

Humans
versus
the Planet
page 93

PACIFIC OCEAN

A L A N T

Revolution
in South
America
page 99

ANTARCTIC

Exploring
the World
page 104

VOTES
FOR
WOMEN
page 93

6 AND THEN...
STEAMING ON

The First Flyers
page 104

During the 19th century the world divided in two. Those who played Industrial Revolution (the Makers) were on one side. Everyone else (the Farmers) was on the other.

The Makers lived mostly in the towns and cities of Europe and North America, working for wages in factories and offices. They discovered medicines and invented machines to make life more comfortable. Many chose their own rulers (democracy). Looking optimistically into the future, they expected things to become better still.

The Farmers dwelled much as their ancestors had done. They made the same living from the land or the seas, caught the same diseases, and worshiped the same gods. The future didn't mean much to them. When things changed, they were surprised.

The Makers of the West used their power to cross to the Farmers' land and take it over. They collected huge empires and provided them with cities and railroads. All for the Farmers' benefit, they said.

Despite their machinery and democracy, the Makers were still human. They argued and squabbled just as humans had always done. So when, in 1914, the Makers set out to blow each other to pieces, for once the Farmers were not surprised at all.

End of the Ottomans
page 96

Preparing
for War
page 105

EUROPE

AFRICA

OCEAN

OCEAN

Dividing
Up Africa
page 100

INDIAN

Napoléon Conquers Europe *page 94*

1800 A.D. TO 1914 A.D.

| 1800 | 1810 | 1820 | 1830 | 1840 |

EUROPE

1804 Napoléon crowns himself Emperor of France (below).

1812 Napoléon invades Russia but is forced to retreat.

1815 Napoléon defeated at Waterloo.

1815 Congress of Vienna follows defeat of Napoléon and decides map of Europe.

1821 Electric motor invented by Michael Faraday.

1820s Romantic movement in European arts: Goethe (German poet, 1749–1832); Byron (British poet, 1788–1824); Turner (British painter, 1775–1851); and Chopin (Polish composer and pianist, 1810–1849).

1826 First photograph produced by Frenchman Niépce.

1825 First passenger steam railroad between Stockton and Darlington in England.

1821–1832 Greek war of independence against Ottoman Turks (right).

1830 Revolts in France, Germany, Poland, and Italy. Belgium wins independence.

1845 Irish famine causes mass Irish emigration to United States.

1840 First postage stamp (Britain).

1848 Communist Manifesto published by Karl Marx.

1848 Revolts across Europe. Second Republic in France.

AFRICA

1814 Cape Colony comes under British control.

1807 Ashanti invade Fante confederation of states.

1807 Slave trade abolished in British Empire, but slavery continues until 1833.

1805–1848 Muhammad Ali takes control in Egypt and breaks away from Ottoman Empire.

1816–28 Shaka forms Zulu Kingdom in Southeast Africa.

1820 Fulani Empire founded in West Africa.

1830 French begin conquest of Algeria.

1832–1847 Abd-al-Kadir leads Arab resistance to French in Algeria.

1836–1837 Great Trek of Boer colonists from Cape Colony, leading to foundation of republics of Natal (1839), Orange Free State (1848) and Transvaal (1849).

ASIA

1819 British found Singapore as free trading port.

1810 King Kamahameha unites Hawaiian Islands.

1802–1820 Emperor Gia-Long unites Vietnam.

1830s First expeditions to explore Antarctica.

1829 Practice of suttee (widow burning) made illegal in India.

1843–1848 British and Maoris fight in New Zealand after British fail to meet terms of Waitangi Treaty.

1839–1842 Opium War between China and Britain: Britain gains Hong Kong island.

AMERICA

1808–1830 Independence movements in South America: 13 states are created by 1828, including Venezuela (1816), Chile (1818), Peru (1821), Brazil (1822), Bolivia (1825), and Uruguay (1828).

1820s Rise of Pacific whaling industry.

1819 United States buys Florida from Spain.

1823 Monroe Doctrine. United States declares that European powers should no longer try to set up colonies in either North or South America.

1838 Trail of Tears. Many thousands of eastern Native Americans are forced to move West, many dying on the way.

1836 Texas gains independence from Mexico.

1846–1848 Mexican War: United States conquers New Mexico and California.

1846 Oregon Treaty sets up United States–Canada boundary.

1849 California Gold Rush (left).

1840 Upper and Lower Canada are united in self-governing union.

850   1860   1870   1880   1890   1900

1854–1856 Crimean War. Russia and Austria fight Turkey, Britain, and France.

Mid-19th century Romantic music continues to flourish with Berlioz (French composer, 1803–1869); Liszt (Polish pianist 1811–1886); Wagner (German composer (1813–1883); Brahms (German composer, 1833–1897), and Verdi (Italian composer, 1813–1901).

1859 Italian-French war against Austria starts Unification of Italy.

1860 Great Age of European novel: Dickens (English, 1812–1870); Dumas (French, 1802–1870); Flaubert (French, 1821–1880); Dostoyevsky (Russian, 1821-1881); Tolstoy (Russian, 1828–1910).

1859 Darwin publishes Origin of Species (right).

1866 Prussia defeats Austria.

1870–1871 Franco-Prussian war leads to Unification of Germany and Third Republic in France.

1874 Emergence of Impressionist school of painting: Monet (French, 1840–1926); Renoir (French, 1841–1919); Degas (French, 1834–1917).

1878 First electric streetlighting (London).

1882 Triple Alliance between Germany, Italy, and Austria-Hungary.

1885 Daimler and Benz build first automobile (Germany).

1895 Italian Marconi invents the wireless (radio).

1904 Anglo-French entente.

1908 Bulgaria becomes independent.

1905 Revolution in Russia, followed by Czarist concessions.

1904–1905 Russo-Japanese War.

1907 Picasso (1881–1973) exhibits first Cubist paintings.

1853–1856 Exploration of David Livingstone in central Africa.

1860 French expansion in West Africa from Senegal.

1873 War between Ashanti and Britain.

1869 Suez Canal opens.

1879 Zulus defeated by British.

1880 Beginning of European scramble for Africa.

1886 Britain and Germany divide up East Africa.

1884 Germany conquers Southwest Africa, Togoland, and the Cameroons.

1890 British begin colonization of Rhodesia (Zimbabwe).

1896 Battle of Adowa: Italians defeated by the Ethiopians.

1899 Boer War begins.

1910 Formation of state of South Africa.

1850–1864 Taiping rebellion in China.

1858 China forced to open ports to foreign powers.

1856 Australia given self-government.

1863 France establishes control over large areas of Southeast Asia, including Cambodia and Laos.

1868–1910 Reign of Rama V, founder of modern Thailand.

1868 Meiji Restoration in Japan. Japan industrializes at a rapid rate.

1885 Foundation of Indian National Congress – campaign for Indian home rule.

1898 United States annexes Hawaii.

1900 Boxer uprising in China.

1906 Revolution in Persia.

1911 Chinese Revolution. End of Qing Dynasty. Sun Yat-Sen becomes first president of the new republic.

1850–1890 Destruction of plains buffalo removes Native Americans' main food supply.

1850 Jeans invented in California.

1862–1890 Last wars against Native Americans in western United States. By 1890, surviving native Americans are confined to small areas.

1867 Canada becomes self-governing.

1861 Outbreak of Civil War.

1867 Russia sells Alaska to the United States.

1865 End of Civil War. Slavery abolished in the United States.

1876 Porfirio Díaz gains control of Mexico. He rules until 1911.

1879 Thomas Edison invents light bulb.

1876 Telephone invented by Alexander Graham Bell.

1877 Thomas Edison invents record-player.

1885 Completion of Canadian Pacific Railroad.

1898 Spanish-American War: United States wins control of Guam, Puerto Rico, and the Philippines. Cuba gains independence.

1914 Panama Canal opened.

1910 Mexican revolution begins.

1903 Wright brothers make first successful gasoline-powered flight.

1913 Henry Ford develops first production assembly of cars.

1905 Einstein's theory of relativity.

BRAINY'S NEW BUDDY

Some super-brainy people found a new god. Unlike the old gods, it didn't seem interested in loving or zapping. It was not a master but a buddy, sent to help bring heaven down to earth. Its name was Science.

CHARLIE'S CHIMPS
The travel craze set us wondering where we had come from. After years of drifting and sifting, Charles Darwin (1809–1882) evolved a new answer: We were not descended from seeds planted in Eden by a gardener god, but from a special species of ape.

With Science at their side, people felt they could do everything. Travel?
They floated in balloons, steamed across (and even under) the oceans in iron ships, and wandered around the countryside in trains.

Communicate? Sticky-stamped letters flitted around the world. Daily newspapers carried news from the four corners of the Earth. Electric messages hummed down telegraph wires, then, thanks to Marconi's radio (1895), through the air itself. One click of a camera (1826) – and grandma scowled on the mantel forever. By 1895, she could be seen walking around on flickering film.

Stay healthy? Clean-fingered doctors began to win the "Battle of Bugs." Surgeons discovered how to cut into bodies without it hurting (*below*). More people learned how to have fun but not babies. Even so, villages swelled to towns and towns to cities. After 8,000 years, *Homo* farmer was slowly making way for a new type of person: *Homo* streetwalker.

Going and Glowing
Karl Benz's gasoline-powered cars (above) started to drive people off the rails in 1885. Meanwhile, the glowing discoveries of Marie Curie (1867–1934, left) first uncovered the mysteries of radiation.

Karl Marx

The most famous prophet of the Great God Science was Karl Marx (1818–1883). He claimed that Science would get rid of money, and make the world perfect. Everyone would own everything equally (Communism). He urged those who already had nothing to take something and divide it up. But many of Marx's followers preferred taking to sharing.

Those in charge of the rich industrial countries set up socialist (semi-Marxist) or liberal (slightly Marxist) governments. These let the people join in government by voting.

New laws tidied up their towns and houses. Citizens were also given vacations (*below*) and a little bit of medicine and schooling. Greater wealth and education made Marxism less attractive to most *Homo* streetwalkers.

BEEF, BRAINS, AND BOSSES
The old gods were "he-men." The new god, Science, was unisex. It taught that just because men were hairier and beefier, they were not better and certainly not brainier. As a result, women started playing men's games, like bossing and voting (New Zealand women voted first, in 1893).

By 1900, it looked as if Science really might make heaven on earth before long, at least for white people.

Every year more of them went to school, took baths, walked through gas-lit streets in leather shoes, ate out of tin cans, and paddled in the ocean. They read novels, watched or played sports, and sang around the piano.

There was a cost, of course. Rivers were poisoned and the air filled with suffocating smoke. Species disappeared. Ignorant lumberjacks and imported rabbits created new deserts of exhausted soil.

But for the time being, it didn't seem to matter. If *Homo* streetwalkers lost their way, they could always ask a policeman – as long as they knew where they were going.

Monster Warning
Mary Shelley's novel Frankenstein (1818) *told the terrifying story of a monster brought to life by electricity* (right). *But her book also warned that science could create as many problems as it solved.*

NAPOLÉON AND CO.

The trouble with cutting off kings' heads is finding something to put in their place. The British tried Oliver Cromwell (page 83), then went back to kings. The French tried governing themselves but ended up with a super-king: the Emperor Napoléon I.

By 1804, Napoléon had made the French the top Europeans with an empire and straight laws and roads. Unfortunately, he didn't know when to stop. He got shipwrecked at Trafalgar (1805) and stuck in the snow in Russia (1812). Finally, the British Duke of Wellington defeated Napoléon at Waterloo (1815), then booted him off to the island of St. Helena before he could cause further trouble.

Napoléon had thrown Europe into the air, then left others to pick up the pieces. New country-making was all the rage.

Cavour taught the Italians they had more in common than they realized, and with Garibaldi's army of 1,000 red shirts (*below*) created Italy (1859–1871). The Danes gave Norway (the Scandinavian hot potato) to the Swedes. They dropped it in 1905 when it became an independent country.

The people of the southern Netherlands set up Belgium in 1830, but couldn't agree on a single language to use.

CHUBBY AND CRAFTY

Chubby Prussian Prime Minister Otto von Bismarck (1815–1898) used blood and iron to defeat his Austrian and French enemies and made a German Empire around Prussia.
Crafty Camillo Cavour (1810–1861) relied on ink and ideas to turn Sardinia into the Kingdom of Italy.

National Beat
As people grew fonder of their country, they liked it to have its own special composer. The Germans chose Ludwig van Beethoven (1770–1827, above middle), the Polish Frederic Chopin (1810–1849, above right), and the Russians Peter Tchaikovsky (1840–1893, above left).

It was all a bit more complicated in the east. The Poles wanted Poland for themselves, but as no one else did they stayed part of Russia. Napoléon had proved there wasn't a Holy Roman Empire, so German-speakers had to decide where they belonged.

Some wanted to shelter with the Hungarians under the Austrian umbrella. Others believed they would be safer snuggling up to Prussia.

MEANWHILE...
While politicians were drawing new boundary lines in Europe, their geographers were ruling Africa into colonies. As African nations didn't live in straight borders, the new lines didn't always make sense.

were still furious at Germany for stealing their favorite provinces, Lorraine and Alsace.

While all this was going on, the British sat rich and smug on their island. Most working people had been lined up in dingy houses and sent to work in factories. Fair-minded people wondered what was going on, and in 1848 radicals (Chartists) demanded change. Prime Minister Gladstone told them to settle down, trust in God, and vote Liberal.

Bismarck made up the Germans' minds for them by defeating Austria (1866) and France (1871). This left the German *kaiser* (emperor) on top of the European dung heap (*above*). To stop Austria and Russia from getting jealous, Bismarck invited them into his League of the Three Emperors.

This advice didn't apply to the Irish, however. When their potatoes ran out in 1845, many were shipped off to become Americans.

After Napoléon I, the French tried a few more Louis and Napoléons until finally they were trampled by Prussia (1871). They set up a Third Republic, and built the Eiffel Tower (1889) to show how proud of it they were. But they

ALSACE

LORRAINE

CARVING THE TURKEY

By 1800, the Turkish Ottoman Empire was dying. Its heart was beating irregularly to the commands of feeble sultans in Constantinople. The Russian bear and the Austrian eagle had already pulled off pieces of European flesh, and the North African limbs were attached by the thinnest threads.

The Egyptians broke free first when Muhammad Ali Pasha made himself sultan (1805, *right*). He and Sultan Abdul Majid set about dragging their country out of its 250-year rut. The Greeks went next. In 1832, cheered on by Britain, France, and Russia (*right*), a new Greece slid onto the world stage.

The Crimean War (1854–1856) started when Britain and France thought the Russian bear was feeding too greedily on Turkey. The war was famous for total incompetence, Balaklava helmets, and a nice woman called Florence Nightingale (1820–1910, *left*) who wandered about Scutari Hospital, looking for wounded men with her lamp.

No one cared much for the patient's suffering, but there was a lot of interest in the body. Greeks, Serbs, and others within the empire wanted to set up on their own. The Russians and Austrians were out to grab what they could for their own empires. (*Left*) Britain and France weren't sure what they wanted, as long as no one else got anything.

RUSSIA
AUSTRIA

DONKEY CHARGE
Although Britannia ruled the waves, she was useless on land. To hide this fact, the poet Tennyson (1809–1892) glorified the Light Brigade's defeat. A French spectator was more honest in describing the soldiers and their officers as "lions led by donkeys."

COMPETITION TIME

The genie from the lamp of Science revealed still more secrets of the universe. Sigmund Freud (1856–1939) told us not to be afraid of our dreams. Science pointed out black holes in space and the ozone layer. It showed us how to split atoms quickly into bombs and slowly into electricity. It even allowed us to play god by making new species.

From the busy workshop of Technology steamed an endless array of inventions. There were strong new metals and flexible new plastics. Travelers were given jet planes, titanic ships, helicopters, and hovercraft. For entertainment came television and other tele-tricks. Most amazing was an electric brain (computer) that could hum through numbers quicker than a thousand professors.

Science, the last great god, now ruled the Earth. Strangely, as its power grew, it began to look more like an ancient zap-god: With one hand it showered blessings, with the other it showered curses. Moreover, good-looking showers (like medicine) often had unpleasant side effects (e.g. overpopulation).

Doctors were the new magicians. They cured the sick with bug-busting drugs and recycled hearts, and beat off disease by sticking pills down throats and needles into bottoms. Smallpox became so tiny it disappeared. But disease was a crafty enemy. By the end of the 20th century, the bugs were fighting back. Since everyone now played Agricultural Revolution, the world was bursting at the seams with people.

1 + 1 = BILLIONS
To avoid breakfast lines stretching from Beijing to Pluto, China's Commie emperors told women to have only one baby. Naturally, it was a hard law to obey.

Penicillin

JEANS AND GREENS

After World War II, a new breed of human appeared – the teenager. It was developed by democrats wanting new consumers. Teenagers tried hard to be themselves, which meant hanging around in herds and looking just like every other teenager – i.e. pimply and quarrelsome. They wore flashy clothes, very long (or short) hair, and obeyed fashion rather than their parents.

Other people started to look and behave more and more like each other, too. Uni-culture music, from Elvis Presley and The Beatles to Jimi Hendrix and Michael Jackson, thumped around the world. Saharan tribes changed 1000-year-old habits to watch T.V. soap operas. Swingers everywhere wore jeans,

Elvis Presley (1935–1977)

MEANWHILE... As films and photographs became more realistic, artists like Pablo Picasso (1881–1973) pointed out that some people looked better with a nose on the side of their face.

Superheroes

Jimi Hendrix (1942–70)

Walt Disney

spoke English, and ate burgers that tasted like rubber.

By the 1990s, *Homo* Streetwalker was supreme. Thriving on noise, crush and rush, it jammed together in "ant-nest" cities. Leisure – once associated with doing nothing in particular – became an industry, led by entertainer Walt Disney (1901–1966) of Hollywood. From the huts of Calcutta to the mansions of Manhattan, the square box in the corner became neighbor, entertainer, teacher, and babysitter.

The new world uni-culture dressed everyone in ready-made suits.

Peaceful prophets like Indian Mahatma Gandhi (1869–1948) and American Martin Luther King (1929–1968) pointed out that all people were also the same inside. This led to "wishful-thinking" laws. These said that all races were equally important and color mattered only on an artist's brush.

Homo streetwalker put individual rights before duties. Men and women (now equal) wanted everything: health, homes, happiness, and their own cars.

BATON CHARGE
When muscle mattered, men conducted the human band. In the modern world, brain was more important than brawn. Women such as Eva Perón (Argentina 1929–1953), Margaret Thatcher (Britain, 1925–), and Indira Gandhi (India, 1917–1984) conducted the "history symphony" just as skillfully as any male maestro.

The age of the gleaming dream machine was born. Camels, horses, bikes, llamas, and even railroad engines stepped aside as *Homo* streetwalkers stopped walking – and drove happily to supermarket heaven.

Mother Earth did not like the way her child, Homo sapiens sapiens, was behaving. It swallowed up her stocks of fish and trees quicker than she could replace them. It polluted her air and her seas.

It bullied its animal brothers and sisters, driving some to extinction. Mother Earth felt hot, dirty, and untidy. Had her super-brainy baby, she wondered, been such a good idea after all?

Sensitive human beings noticed the Earth's distress. They felt guilty and anxious. Their history was now at a vital crossroads. It could go on only when (and if) the light turned green.

Hoping they hadn't left it too late, people began to cut down their smoking, *(right)* chat with whales, and re-cycle the mess in their backyard.

TIGER TIME

By 1990, the bankrupt Soviet Union had disappeared down the drain of history.

The Cold War melted and the iron curtain rusted away. Poles, Russians, Czechs, Slovaks, Bulgarians, Ukrainians, etc., stopped being comrades, joined the democrats, and followed Western-style competition and crime. Uncle Sam was left to police the world alone.

The Japanese had vanished beneath a pile of rubble in 1945. Down but not out, they picked themselves up and joined the democrats. Hard work was in, wasting money on guns was out. Soon the young tigers of trade were flooding market stalls from Chicago to Calcutta with their reliable radios, T.V.s, cameras, and cars.

The roar of the Japanese tiger echoed around the Pacific Rim. Hearing it, the young tigers of Hong Kong, Taiwan, Korea, Singapore, and Malaysia created their own flood of products. The noise impressed even the Chinese.

They broke the Commie Rule and entered (and won) competitions for making bicycles and other cheap goods.

The American dream had become a nightmare. The United States had spent its dollars on wars, the Arabs had refused to fill up its gas guzzlers, and President Richard Nixon had turned out to be less than honest. Afro-Americans said that 200 years after the revolution, they still hadn't been given their rights. Overseas, fast-growing Asian countries, "Asian Tigers," were learning to beat the U.S. at its own competitions.

ROCKER AND SHOCKER
The world was rocked by the assassination of President John F. Kennedy (left) *in 1963.*

Sri Lankan Sirimavo Bandaranaike (born 1916, right) shocked the political world by becoming the first woman prime minister in 1960.

Afraid of the tigers, Australians and New Zealanders drew closer to the United States. Meanwhile, governing India was so difficult that for a while only the handy Gandhis – Mahatma, Indira, and Rajiv (1944–1991) – could cope. Their successors encouraged their people to become young tigers.

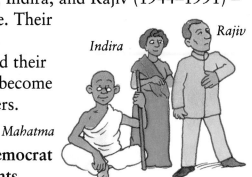

Indira

Rajiv

Mahatma

Africa's democrat governments weren't successful because the people weren't used to competition. In Uganda, Idi Amin's mean lot, trained in the West, showed them. Other African leaders wrote their own newspapers and banned competition. Things improved in the south, where Nelson Mandela (born 1918) created a rainbow nation of Boers and Africans in 1994 (*left*).

Central and South Americans paid their debts by teaching the rest of the world to play soccer. They divided their time off the field between carnivals and wrestling with nasty dictators.

BEWARE OF COMPETITION

Two of the West's gifts to the world – countries and competitions – proved to be booby traps (*above*). New countries meant new squabbles (e.g. in Russia, Bosnia, and Rwanda). Competitions to make fast and sell quick overheated and poisoned the planet. Human tigers were killing off the real ones.

By the end of the 20th century, some believers (especially Muslims) said the West's gods were false and we should go back to the old ones. But they couldn't agree on which ones, or how to worship them. Despite their big heads, super-brainy people still hadn't found all the answers!

WELL, WELL, WELL...
In 1973, the Arabs realized the answer to the Palestine problem lay under their noses. When the sheikhs switched off their oil pumps, millions of motorists thought it was time for the Arabs and Israelis to stop fighting and start gassing.

STILL SMILING

Homo sapiens sapiens traveled a long, long way in 40,000 years. Their destination was always heaven. Unfortunately, lacking a reliable map, they were never quite sure where heaven was. Some said it was in the clouds, others said it was over the next hill.

As a result, the travelers spent much of their time going round in circles and ending up where they had started. Every now and again, however, they followed the sign posts of zap-gods, holy men, or science and stumbled a few steps nearer their distant goal.

Looking back, they gazed in wonder at what they had been through.

There were pieces of broken empire, memories of deeds great and bad, shattered dreams, fragments of fine ideas and inventions, and ghosts of billions of ordinary lives. Some of the time-worn debris looked beautiful, other pieces were best forgotten.

People showed a remarkable ability to adapt along the way. Starting as hairy hunters, they turned themselves into farmers, then streetwalkers. Flood, famine, war, pollution – nothing could stop them. After each setback, they picked themselves up, dusted themselves off and set out again, still with a smile on their lips and a spring in their step.

Human beings still don't know where heaven is. But they are determined to press on until they get there.

And then… ?

INDEX

Abbas I, Shah of Persia 67
Abdul Majid, Sultan of Egypt 96
Adenan people 25
Afghans/Afghanistan 78, 101, 117
Africa 24, 42, 63, 68-69, 76-77, 100-101, 118, 123, *see also* individual countries
Ahmad, Chief of Durrani, Afghanistan 78
Ainu people 49
Akbar I, Emperor (India) 66
Aksumites 24, 42
Alans 38
Alexander III, Czar of Russia 97
Alexander the Great, King of Macedon (northern Greece) 23, 30
Algeria 76
Ali Bey, Sultan of Algiers 76
Ali the Zanj 40
Allah (Islamic god) 40, 69
Amaterasu (Japanese goddess) 26
America
  Central 25, 50, 62-3, 99, 123
  North 25, 50, 63, 74-5, 84, 98
  South 25, 51, 60, 62, 63, 99, 123
  see also individual countries
Americans, Native 13, 25, 74, 98
  see also Adenan, Hohokam, Hopewells, Inuit, Mississippi and Mogollon people.

Amin, Idi, President of Uganda 123
Anasazi people 50
Andropov, Leonid, Soviet Premier 112
Arabs 40-1, 42, 44, 68, 76, 114, 117, 122, 123
Arawak people 75
Armstrong, Neil 118
Aryan peoples 23
Asaf Jah, Nizam of Hyderabad 79
Ashanti people 77, 100
Ashurbanipal, King of Assyria 28
Asia – *see* individual countries
Asoka, Emperor (India) 23
Assyrians 24, 28
Augustus, Emperor of Rome 31

Aurungzeb, Emperor (India) 66, 79
Australia 13, 81, 103, 115, 123
  Aborigines 103
Australopithecines 10
Austrians/Austria 61, 78, 95, 96, 105, 110
Avars 38
Aztecs 62, 63

Babar, Emperor (India) 66
Babylonians/Babylon 20, 31
Bacon, Roger 57
Bacon, Sir Francis 56
Bandaranaike, Sirimavo, Prime Minister of Sri Lanka 122
Bantu people 42
Basil II, Emperor of Byzantium 43
Bathild, Saint 38
Bayinnaung, King of Burma 65
Bede, Venerable 38
Beethoven, Ludwig van 94
Belgians/Belgium 94
Benin 77
Benz, Karl 92
Berber people 42
Bismarck, Otto von, Prime Minister of Prussia and Germany 94, 95, 105
Boers 76, 100, 123
Boleslav I, Duke of Bohemia 39
Bolívar, Simón 99
Bolivia 99
Borgia family (Italy) 59
Brazil 99
Britain 39, 58, 59, 60, 61, 74, 75, 79, 82, 83, 84, 94, 94, 95, 96, 97, 98, 100-01, 104-05, 110, 114-5
Bruce, James 77
Buddha (Gautama) 23, 33
Bulgars/Bulgaria 43, 58, 97, 122
Burma (Myanmar) 48, 81, 101
Byzantines/Byzantium 43, 58

Caesar, Julius 5, 17, 31
Caligula, Emperor of Rome 31
Cambodia 48, 101
Canadians/Canada 74, 98, *see also* North America
Capone, Al 111
Carib people 75
Castro, Fidel, President of Cuba 116
cathedrals 33, 39, 47
Catherine II, "the Great," Czarina of Russia 82, 83
Cavour, Camillo di 94
Celts 29, 31
Cervantes, Miguel de 82
Chamberlain, Neville, Prime Minister of Britain 114

Chandara Gupta, Emperor (Gupta) 23
Chandaragupta, Emperor (Maurya) 23
Charlemagne, King of the Franks, Holy Roman Emperor 38, 41
Charles I, King of England 83
Charles II, King of England 83
Charles V, Holy Roman Emperor 61
Charles XII, King of Sweden 82
Chavín people 25
Chimu people 51
Chiang Kai-Shek 113
Chinese/China 22, 45, 46, 49, 64, 80, 102, 104, 113, 114-5, 116
Cholas 44
Chopin, Frédéric 94
Churchill, Sir Winston, Prime Minister of Britain 114, 115
Cleopatra, Queen of Egypt 21
Clive, Robert 79
Columbus, Christopher 5, 60
Confucius 22, 32, 33, 65
Constantine I, "the Great," Emperor of Rome 33, 43
Cook, James 81
Copernicus, Nicolaus 56
Cornwallis, General Charles 84
Cortés, Hernan 63
Cromwell, Oliver 83, 94
Cuba 99, 116
Curie, Marie 92
Czechoslovakia 110, 114, 117, 122

Darby, Abraham 87
Darius the Great, King of Persia 30
Darwin, Charles 92
Deng Xiao-ping, Chairman (China) 113
Denmark 39, 94
Díaz, Porfirio 99
Dickens, Charles 95
Dinosaurs 9
Disney, Walt 120
"Dorado, El" 60
Dumas, Alexandre 82
Dutch/Holland/Netherlands 59, 60, 61, 76, 82, 100

Edison, Thomas 98
Edward VII, King of England 105
Egypt/Egyptians
  ancient 21, 24, 25, 28, modern 76, 96, 100, 101
Elizabeth I, Queen of England 61
Environmental issues 93, 121
Ethiopians/Ethiopia 24, 42, 69, 77, 101
European Community 118
Europe – *see* individual countries
Explorers 60

Fatimid caliphs 42
Ferdinand VII, King of Spain 99
Francis I, King of France 61

Franco, General Francisco 114
France 39, 58, 60, 74, 79, 82, 83, 85, 94, 95, 96, 97, 98, 99, 100, 101, 105, 110, 114-5, *see also* Franks
Frankenstein (Mary Shelley) 10, 93
Franks 38
Franz Ferdinand, Archduke of Austria 105
Frederick II the Great, King of Prussia 82, 83
Freud, Sigmund 119
Fujiwara clan 49
Fulani people 100

Gagarin, Yuri 112
Galileo Galilei 56
Galvani, Luigi 86
Gandhi, Indira, Prime Minister of India 121, 123
Gandhi, Mahatma 121, 123
Gandhi, Rajiv, Prime Minister of India 123
Garibaldi, Giuseppe 94
Gautama, Siddhartha (Buddha) 23, 33
Genghis Khan, King of All the Mongols 46
George III, King of England 84
Germans/Germany 58, 61, 82, 95, 104-5, 110, 111, 112, 114-5, 116, *see also* Prussia
Ghana 42, 77
Gia-Long, Emperor of Vietnam 101
Gilgamesh, Epic of 20
Gladstone, William Ewart, Prime Minister of Britain 95
Gogh, Vincent van 104
Golden Horde 66
Gorbachev, Mikhail, Soviet Premier 112
Goths 38
Greeks/Greece
  ancient 28, 30
  modern 96
Gupta Empire (India) 23, 44
Gutenberg, Johannes 56

Hammurabi, King of Babylon 20
Han Dynasty (China) 22, 35, 45
Harappa/Harappans 23
Harun al-Rashid, Caliph of Baghdad 41
Harvey, William 56
Hatshepsut, Queen of Egypt 21
Hattushili, King of the Hittites 28
Hebrew people 28
Heraclius, "the Hero," Emperor of Byzantium 43
Hidalgo, Miguel 99
Hideyoshi Toyotomi 65
Hitler, Adolf, 114-115, 117
Hittite people 20, 27, 28
Ho Chi Minh, President of Vietnam 116

Hohokam people 50
Homo 10, 24
  Homo erectus 10-11
  Homo habilis 10
  Homo sapiens 11-12
  Homo sapiens neanderthalensis 11, 12
  Homo sapiens sapiens 11-12, 124-125
Hong Kong 102, 122
Hong Xiuquan 102
Hopewell people 50
Huari people 51
Huitzilopochtli (Aztec god) 62
Hungarians/Hungary 39, 58, 61, 95, 117, 122
Huns 38, 46

Incas 51, 62, 63, 75
Indians/India 23, 44, 60, 66, 78-9, 101, 114, 117, 123, *see also* Gupta Empire, Mauryan Empire, Moghul Dynasty
Inuit people 25, 50, 74
Inventions 27, 47, 56-7, 86-7, 92-3, 118-9
Ireland/Irish 95
Isis (Egyptian goddess) 21, 26
Ismail I, Shah of Persia 67
Israel 117, *see also* Jews
Italians/Italy 31, 38, 58, 59, 94, 114
Ivan IV, "the Terrible," Czar of Russia 61
Izz Ad-Din Abu Al-Mansur, Sultan of Delhi 44

Jaganath (Hindu god) 79
Jahangir, Emperor (India) 66
James I, King of England 83
James II, King of England 83
Japanese/Japan 26, 49, 65, 81, 103, 113, 114-5, 118, 122
Jenner, Dr. Edward 86
Jesus 33
Jews 32, 33, 58, 114, 115, 117
Jimmu, Emperor of Japan 26
Jomon culture 26
Jurchen people 45

Kalidasa (poet) 44
Kang-Hsi, Emperor of China 80
Kennedy, John F., President of the United States 122
Khmer people 48
Khoisan people 21, 24
Kim Il Sung, President of North Korea 116
King, Martin Luther 121
Koreans/Korea 48, 65, 102, 116, 122
Kublai Khan, Emperor of China 45, 49
Kumasi 77
Kushites 24

Lanzon (god) 25
Lavoisier, Antoine 86
Leeuwenhoek, Anton van 56
Lenin, Vladimir, Soviet Premier 112, 113
Leonardo da Vinci 59
Lincoln, Abraham, President of the United States 98

Linnaeus, Carolus 86
Lithuania 58
Louis V, "Lazybones," King of France 39
Louis XIV, "the Sun King" of France 82
Louis XVI, King of France 85
L'Ouverture, Toussaint 99
Lubalanders 69
"Lucy" 10
Lunda people 77

Malays/Malaysia 26, 101, 122
Mali 42, 68
Mamelukes 46, 66
Manchu people/Manchuria 45, 64, 80, 102
Mandela, Nelson, President of South Africa 123
Mao Zedong, Chairman (China) 113
Maori people 48, 65, 81, 103
Maratha people 78, 79
Marconi, Guglielmo 92
Marie Antoinette, Queen of France 85
Marlborough, 1st Duke of 82
Marx, Karl/Marxism 93, 112-113
Massagetae 13
Mauryan Empire 23
Mayas 50-51
Menes, King of Egypt 21
Mercator, Gerardus 57
Mexicans/Mexico 99, *see also* Aztecs
Minamoto clan 49
Ming Dynasty (China) 64
Minoans 28, 29
Mississippi people 50
Mogollon people 25
Mogul Dynasty (India) 66, 67, 78-79
Monet, Claude 105
Mongols 35, 45, 46, 46, 49, 58, 60, 64, 65, 66
Montgolfier, Joseph and Jacques 87
Moroccans/Morocco 68, 76
Mozart, Wolfgang Amadeus 83
Muhammad (Islamic prophet) 40, 42
Muhammad Ali, Sultan of Egypt 96
Muhammad II, "the Conqueror," Sultan of Turkey 67
Muhammad Turré, King of Songhai 68
Mumtaz Mahal 66
Mussolini, Benito 114
Mycenae/Mycenaeans 28

Nader Kuli, Shah of Persia 78-79
Nanak, Guru 66
Napoléon I Bonaparte, Emperor of France 85, 94, 95
Neanderthals 11, 12
Newton, Sir Isaac 86
New Zealand 48, 65, 81, 103, 115

Nicholas II, Czar of Russia 97, 112
Nightingale, Florence 96
Nixon, Richard, President of the United States 122
Nok people 24
Norwegians/Norway 94
Nzinga, Queen of Ndongo 69

Olmec people 25
Osei Tutu, King of the Ashanti 77
Osman I, Sultan of Turkey 67
Ottomans 61, 67, 69, 76, 78, 79, 96-97, 105

Pachacuti, Sapa-Inca of Peru 62
Pakistan 117, see also Harappa
Palestine 117
Pallava Dynasty (India) 44
Pedro II, Emperor of Brazil 99
Perón, Eva 121
Persia (Iran) 30, 43, 67, 78-9, 101
Peru 99, see also Incas
Peter I the Great, Czar of Russia 82
Philip II, King of Spain 61
Phoenician people 28
Phya Taksin, General (Thailand) 81
Picts 38
Pilgrim Fathers 63
Pitt, William, the Elder, Prime Minister of Britain 74
Pizarro, Francisco 63
Poles/Poland 58, 61, 82, 95, 114, 122
Polo, Marco 60
Polynesian peoples 26, 35, 48, 60, 81
Portuguese/Portugal 60, 68-9, 75, 100
Prince Regent, (later George IV of England) 80
Princip, Gavrilo 105
Prussians/Prussia 74, 82, 83, 94, 95
Pu Yi, Emperor of China 102

Qianlong, Emperor of China 80
Qin Dynasty (China) 22
Quetzalcoatl (Aztec and Maya god) 51, 62

Rajaraja I, King of Cholas (India) 44
Rajendra I, King of Cholas (India) 44
Rama (Hindu god) 66
Rama I, King of Thailand 81
Rama V, King of Thailand 101

Rasputin, Grigoriy 112
Religion 32-33, 40, 58-9, 66
Rhodes, Cecil 100
Robespierre, Maximilien de 85
Roderick, King of Spain 40
Rodin, Auguste 105
Rome
ancient 23, 30-1, 38, 43
Russians/Russia 39, 58, 61, 78, 82, 83, 94, 96-7, 102, 104-5, 110, 112, 122, see also Soviet Union

Safanid Dynasty (Persia) 67, 78
Samuel, Czar of the Bulgars 43
Sassanid kings (Persia) 43
Scottish/Scotland 29, 39, 58, 61
Serbia 105
Severus, Septimius, Emperor of Rome 24
Shah Jahan I, Emperor (India) 66
Shaka, King of the Zulus 100
Shakespeare, William 59
Shang Dynasty (China) 22, 27
Shelley, Mary 93
Shunzhi, Emperor of China 80
Singapore 122
Siuraj-ud-Dawlah, Nawab of Bengal 79
Sivaji I, Maratha King 79
Slavs 38
Songhai Empire 68
Sonni Ali, King of Songhai 68
Soviet Union 112, 114-5, 116-7, 122, see also Russia
Spanish/Spain 40, 58, 60, 61, 75, 100, 114
Stalin (Joseph Dzhugashvili) 112, 114, 115
Sudan 24, 100, see also Kushites
Suleiman II the Magnificent, Emperor of Turkey 61, 67
Sumerians/Sumer 14, 15, 20, 21, 23, 27, 68
Sun Yat Sen 102
Suppululiumas, King of the Hittites 28
Surya (Indian god) 32
Swedes/Sweden 61, 82, 94
Swiss/Switzerland 82

Tabinshwehti, King of Burma 65
Taiwanese/Taiwan 80, 122
Tang Dynasty (China) 45, 49
Tariq (Muslim general) 40
Tchaikovsky, Peter 94, 97
Tennyson, Alfred, Lord 96
Thai people/Thailand (Siam) 65, 81, 101
Thatcher, Margaret, Prime Minister of Britain 121
Tiahuanaco people 51
Timur Lenk 66, 67
Tipu Sultan, Sultan of Mysore 79
Tojo, General Hideki, Premier of Japan 115
Tokugawa clan 65
Tolstoy, Leo 97
Toulouse-Lautrec, Henri de 104
Trailok, King of Siam (Thailand) 65
Trotsky, Leon 112

Tu, Emperor (China) 22
Tupac Amaru 75
Turks/Turkey 40-41, 44, 46, 66, 78, 96-97, 105
capture of Constantinople 43, 67
Mamelukes 46, 66
at Vienna 61, 67
see also Ottomans

Ubaydullah, Caliph of Fatimid Empire 42
United States of America 84, 98, 99, 110, 111, 114-5, 116-7, 118, 122, see also North America

Vandals 38, 43, 46
Victoria, Queen of England 98, 101, 103
Vietnamese/Vietnam 101, 116
Vikings 38, 39, 51, 57
Vladimir I, Saint, King of the Rus 39
Voltaire, François Arouet de 83

Wales 58
Washington, George, President of the United States 85
Watt, James 87
Wellington, 1st Duke of 94
Wen di, Emperor of China 45
Wenceslas I, Saint, Duke of Bohemia 39
William III, of Orange, King of England 83
Wilson, Woodrow, President of the United States 111
Wolfe, General James 74
Wordsworth, William 87
World War I 110
World War II 115
Wright, Orville and Wilbur 104

Xia Dynasty (China) 22

Yi Dynasty (Korea) 65
Yi Song-gye, Emperor of Korea 65
Yong Le, Emperor of China 64
Yongzheng, Emperor of China 80

Yuan Dynasty (China) 45
Yuan Shikai 113

Zeus (ancient Greek god) 33
Zheng He 60, 64
Zhu Yuanzhang, Emperor of China 64
Zimbabwe 69
Zozimus (historian) 33
Zulu people 100

PRINTED IN BELGIUM BY proost INTERNATIONAL BOOK PRODUCTION